Images to Read
Imágenes para Leer

Eduardo Machuca-Torres

Images to Read
Eduardo Machuca-Torres

PHOTOGRAPHS

Eduardo Machuca-Torres

WALL POEMS

Armando Alanís-Pulido

POEMS' ENGLISH TRANSLATION

Eduardo Machuca-Torres

INTERIOR BOOK DESIGN

Eduardo Machuca-Torres

BOOK COVER DESIGN

CreateSpace

POEMS READABILITY

Flesch reading ease score:	96.5
Flesch-Kincaid grade level:	1.3
Automated readability index:	0.1
Coleman-Liau index:	2.4
Gunning-Fog index:	4.2
SMOG index:	5.9

ISBN: 1453633189

EAN-13: 9781453633182

Photographs Information

Printed images are on permanent exhibit at:

La Nacional, Cantina-Restaurant
Calzada Madero 1160
Centro
Monterrey, Nuevo Leon, Mexico
Phone: +52(81)8375-3890

Images exhibited on:

The International Book Fair 2007,
during The Universal Forum of Cultures Monterrey 2007
Cintermex - Parque Fundidora
Monterrey, Nuevo Leon, Mexico

To order prints, please go to:

http://tinyurl.com/images-to-read

* The image above is a QR Code, to be read with camera-equipped cellular phones and QR Code Reader software. There is free QR Code Reader software for your phone on the internet or with your cell phone manufacturer or mobile service provider.

About Eduardo Machuca-Torres

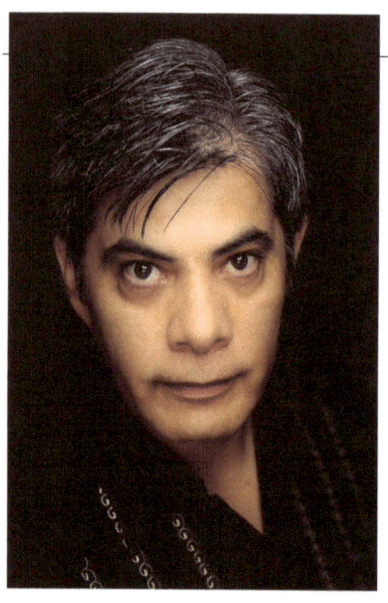

Eduardo Machuca-Torres (1966, Tuxpam, Veracruz, Mexico) holds a engineering degree in electronics and telecommunications (ITESM '88), a master's degree in business leadership (Duxx '96), and worked for many years in the telecommunications and information technology industries and co-founded an embedded systems design firm. All in Monterrey, Mexico.

He started learning photography at around age 12. Even though the camera never left his hand since then, he switched careers and turned a full-time professional photographer until age 39.

He is now a wedding and portrait photographer working mainly in Cancun and the Mayan Riviera. He lives in Merida, Yucatan, Mexico. His photography work has been exhibited and published. He has taught workshops and university courses on photography.

About Armando Alanís-Pulido

Armando Alanís-Pulido (1969, Monterrey, Nuevo Leon, Mexico) was a scholarship holder at the *Centro de Escritores de Nuevo León* (Nuevo Leon's Writers Center) during 1995-1996, and was a member of the *Consejo para la Cultura de Nuevo* León (Advisory Board for Nuevo Leon's Culture).

He received the *Premio Nacional de Poesía Jóven "Ubaldo Ramos"* ("Ubaldo Ramos" National Award for Young Poets) in 1998. He is the founder of the group *Acción Poética* (Poetic Action). From 1993 to 2003, Armando has published 10 poetry books.

Dedication

To my mother who has been there for us,

to my father[†] who taught me photography,

to my son who is my pride.

To my family and friends and clients.

Table of Contents

What does your heart says?_____01

I am weak before my weakness_____02

I breathe your name_____03

I exist when I think of you_____04

Sometimes I get assaulted by your perfume_____05

I keep what you gave me without giving me nothing_____06

An urgent kiss in the silence_____07

Your smile decorates the afternoon_____08

We are an interval between two absences_____09

We are instants_____10

Beware of yourself_____11

It doesn't matter who you are, destiny will find you_____12

I still belong to myself_____13

May my soul have no rest, if loving is about_____14

I dreamed that you wanted me_____15

To be alone is not by chance_____16

You empty the emptiness_____17

You and I, from heaven to heaven_____18

The world is born when two kiss each other_____19

If you were two, which one would win?_____20

I'm the one who has lost the rest in your attainable sum_____21

There is still much left to be felt_____22

And if I eat you to kisses?_____23

You deserve what you dream_____24

Imagine yourself in love_____25

We are the words that say who we are_____26

I believe in love because I am never satisfied_____27

Tell a taxicab to follow you thoughts_____28

Land in my arms_____29

To flourish by looking into your eyes_____30

Are you coming or should I go? _____31

Your mouth convokes_____32

We are the evidence_____33

Not looking at you is the greatest disaster_____34

I am your gaze that observes me_____35

It all begins at your lips_____36

Sunrise, La Silla hill_____37

Introduction

It was the Summer of 2005 when Felipe Chapa, friend and owner of an upscale Mexican cantina-restaurant, commissioned me to make photographs of the street poetry works of Armando Alanís-Pulido and his group *Acción Poética* (Poetic Action), in Monterrey, Nuevo Leon, Mexico.

Armando Alanís has been painting unused street walls with white, and writing with black paint short poetic verses on them. He has been doing this for more than 14 years; he turned 10 years on 2006. In that 10-years time frame, he painted and wrote short poems on over 3500 street walls and should be close to 5,000 by now.

"Words get carried away with the wind", but also written walls. Every time there are political elections, every time a popular event is in town, be it a a musical group or a circus, then those walls get painted over to advertise the event in turn. And when those events end, Armando's work starts again.

The wall and poem you see here today, may not be there by tomorrow. But the poem will show up somewhere else, in another wall in the city. And the wall that used to hold the first poem, may also show up again another day, with another phrase on it. Thus, when Armando's project is seen as a whole, it resembles a living organism; following the city's bloodstream.

In Armando's own words, *"The city is a poem with never-ending verses, just like its streets"*.

My work, as a photographer, was to make images out of Armando's work. Not to take snapshots of the walls. So, these 36 images are an interpretation, as seen through my eyes, and camera.

Eduardo Machuca-Torres

July 2010, Merida, Yucatan, Mexico

This page intentionally left blank

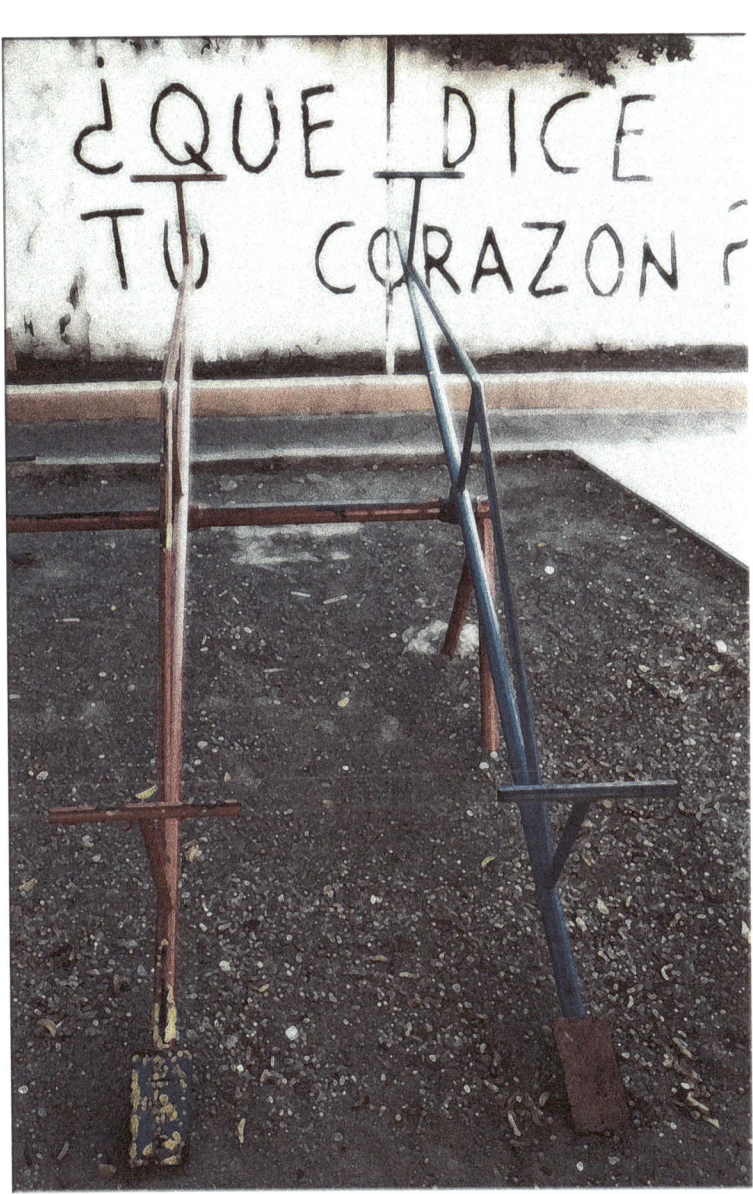

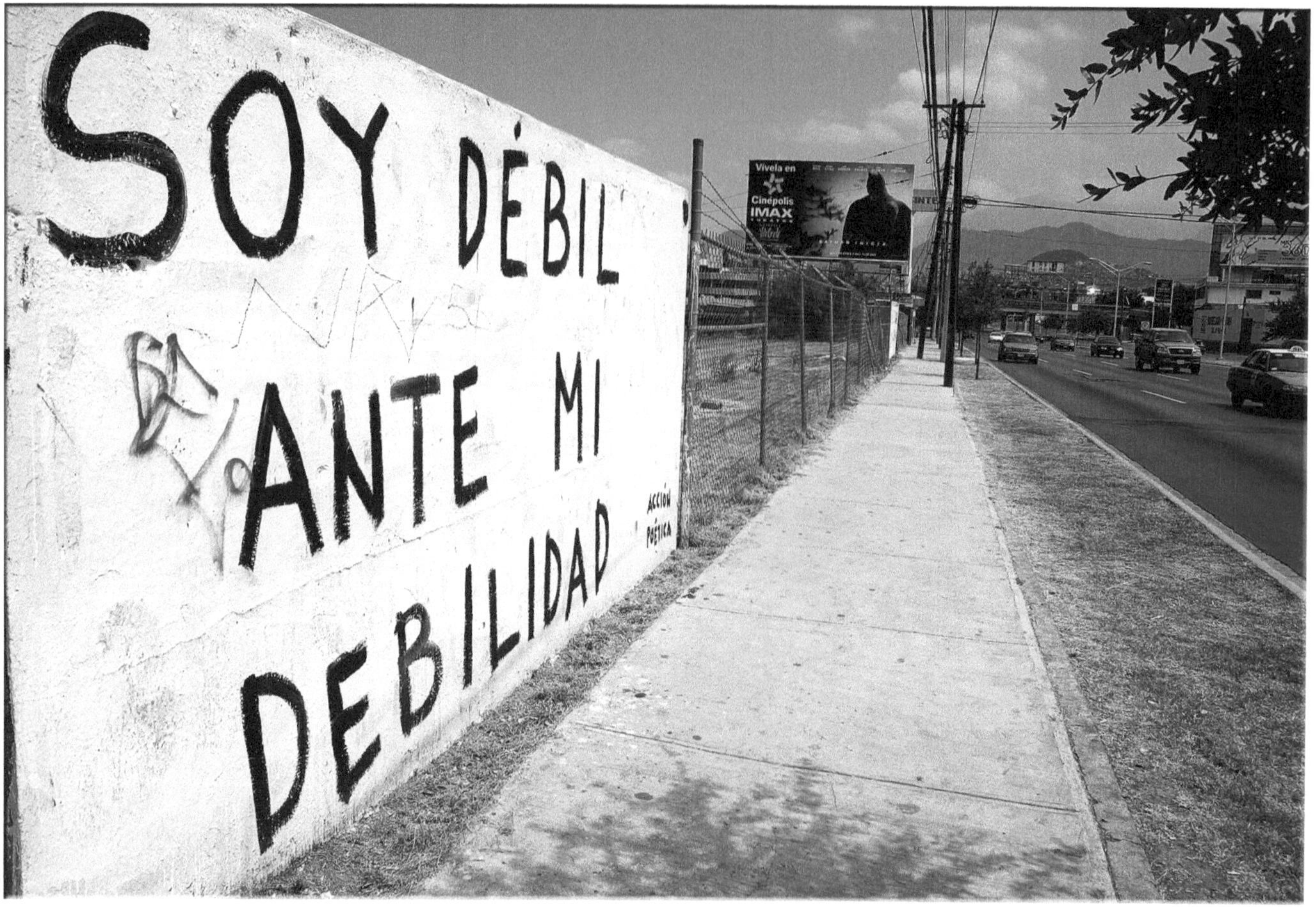
SOY DÉBIL
ANTE MI
DEBILIDAD
ACCIÓN
POÉTICA
Vívela en
Cinépolis
IMAX

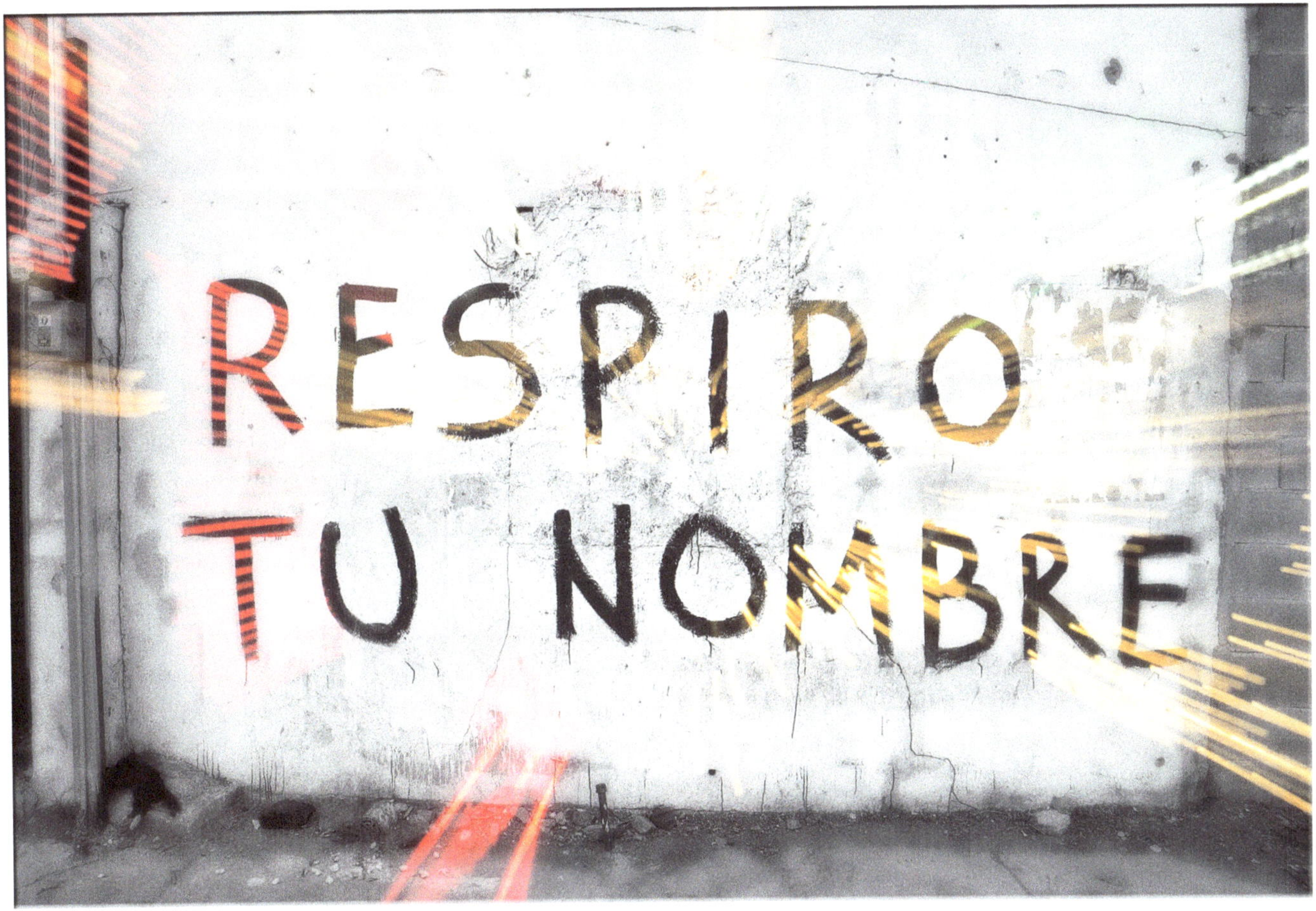
RESPIRO
TU NOMBRE

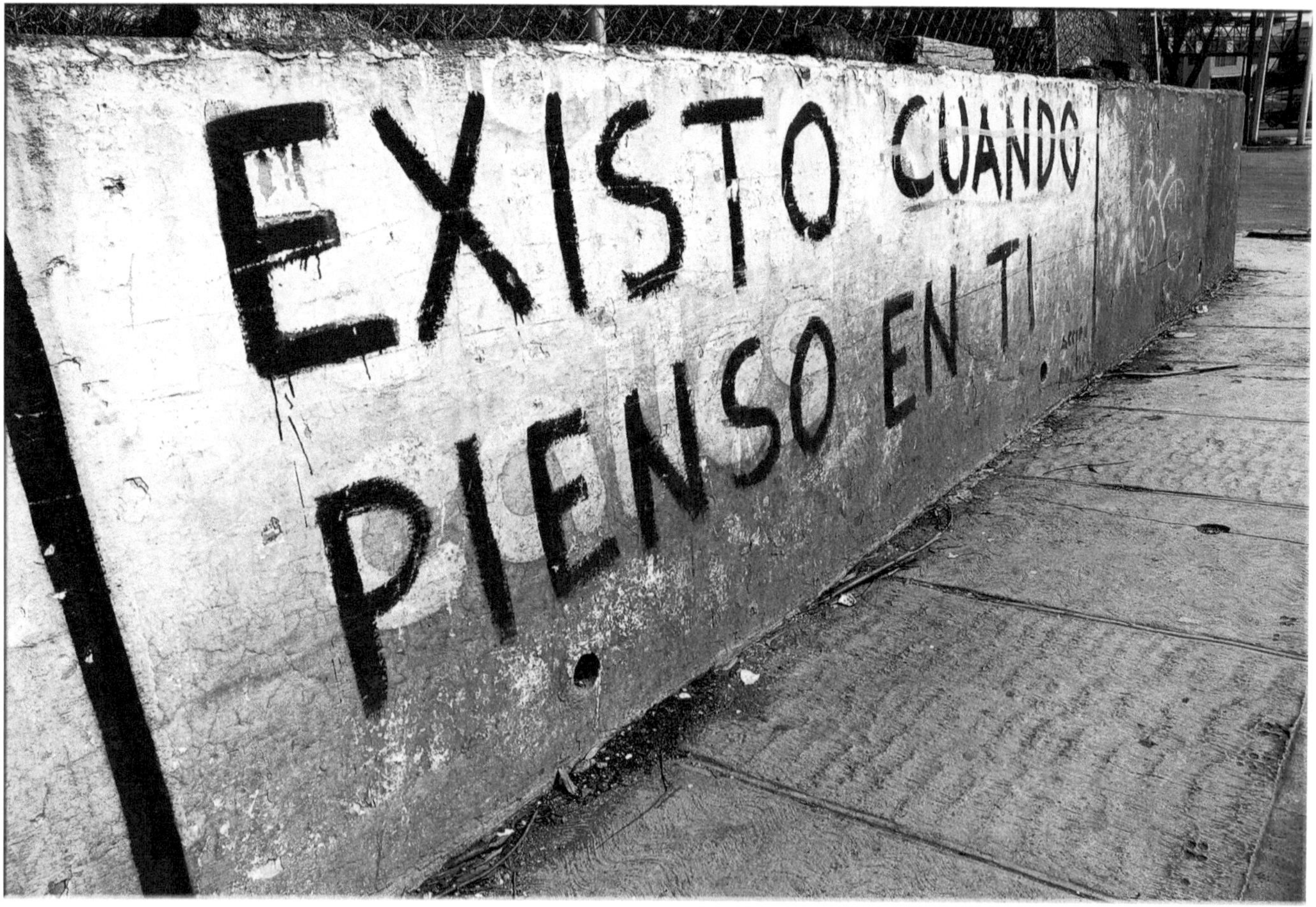
EXISTO CUANDO
PIENSO EN TI.

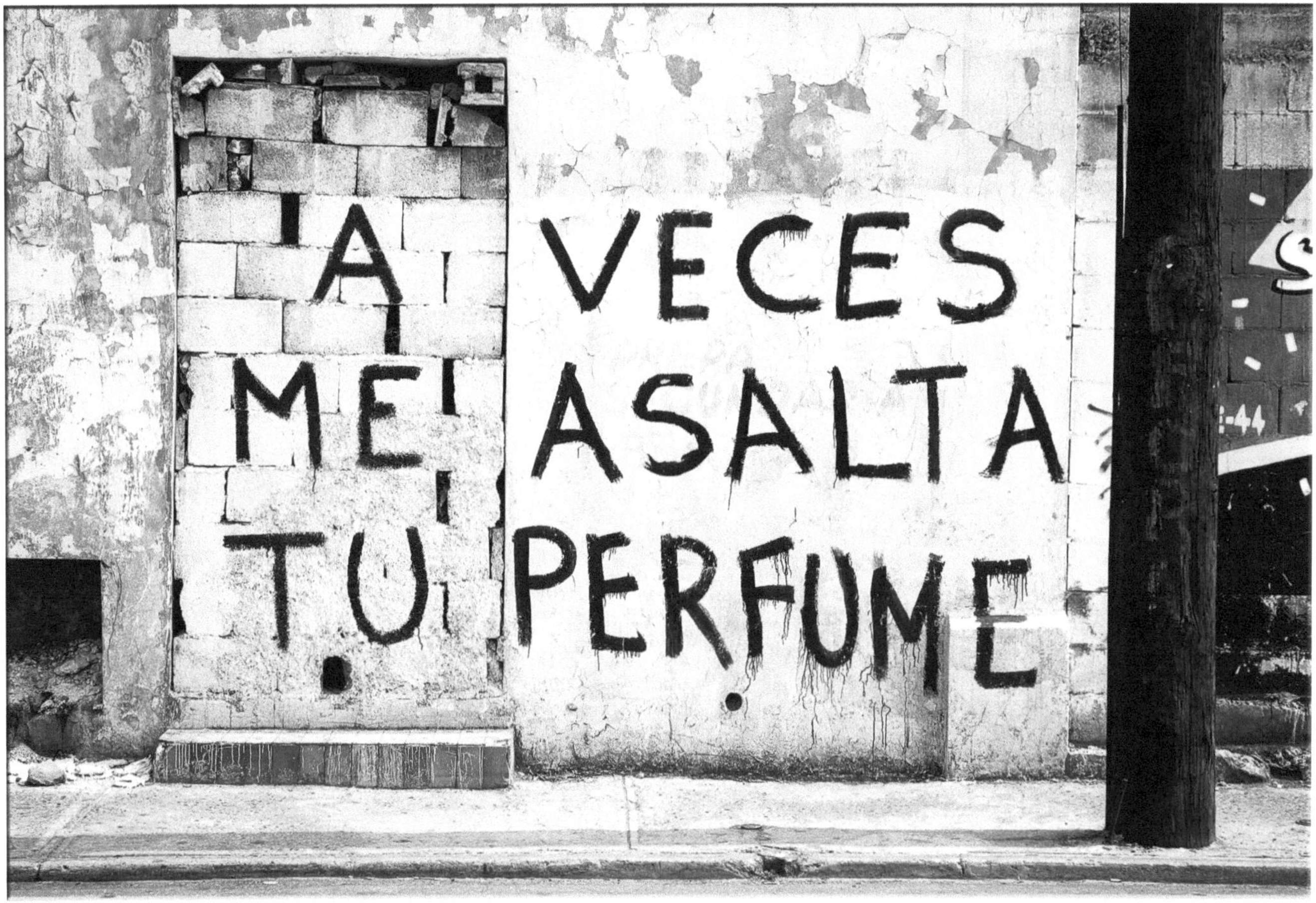
A VECES
ME ASALTA
TU PERFUME

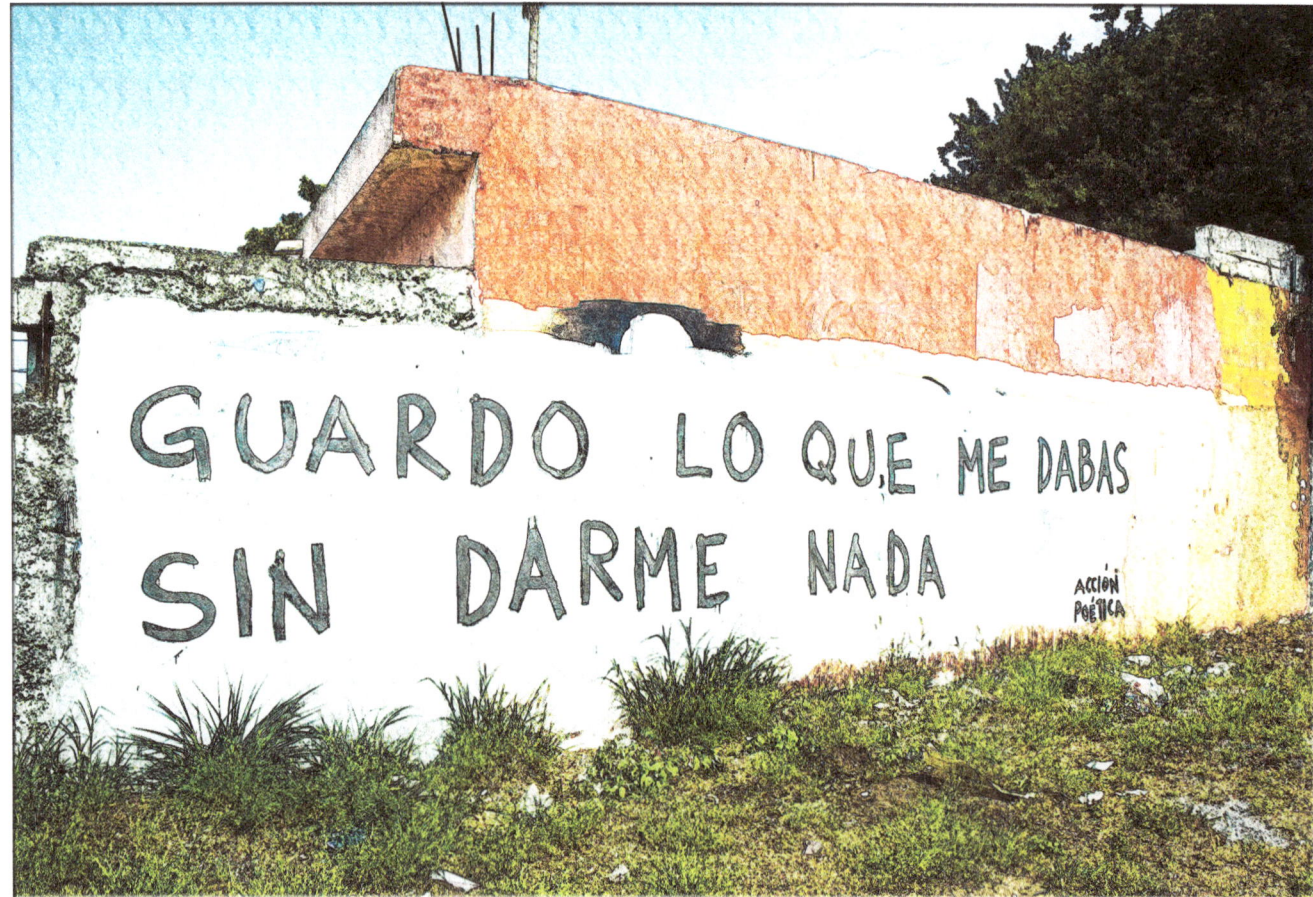

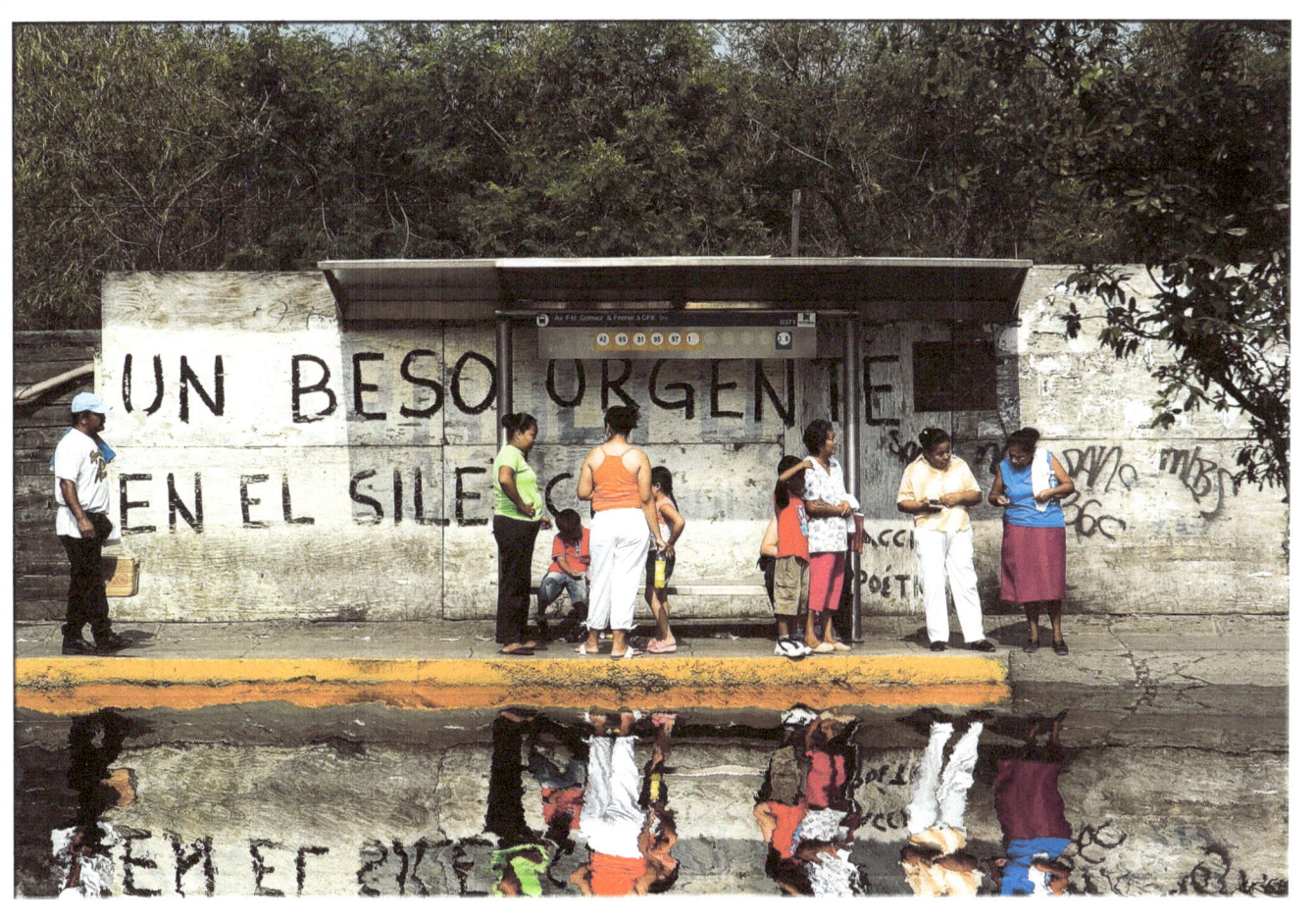

An urgent kiss in the silence

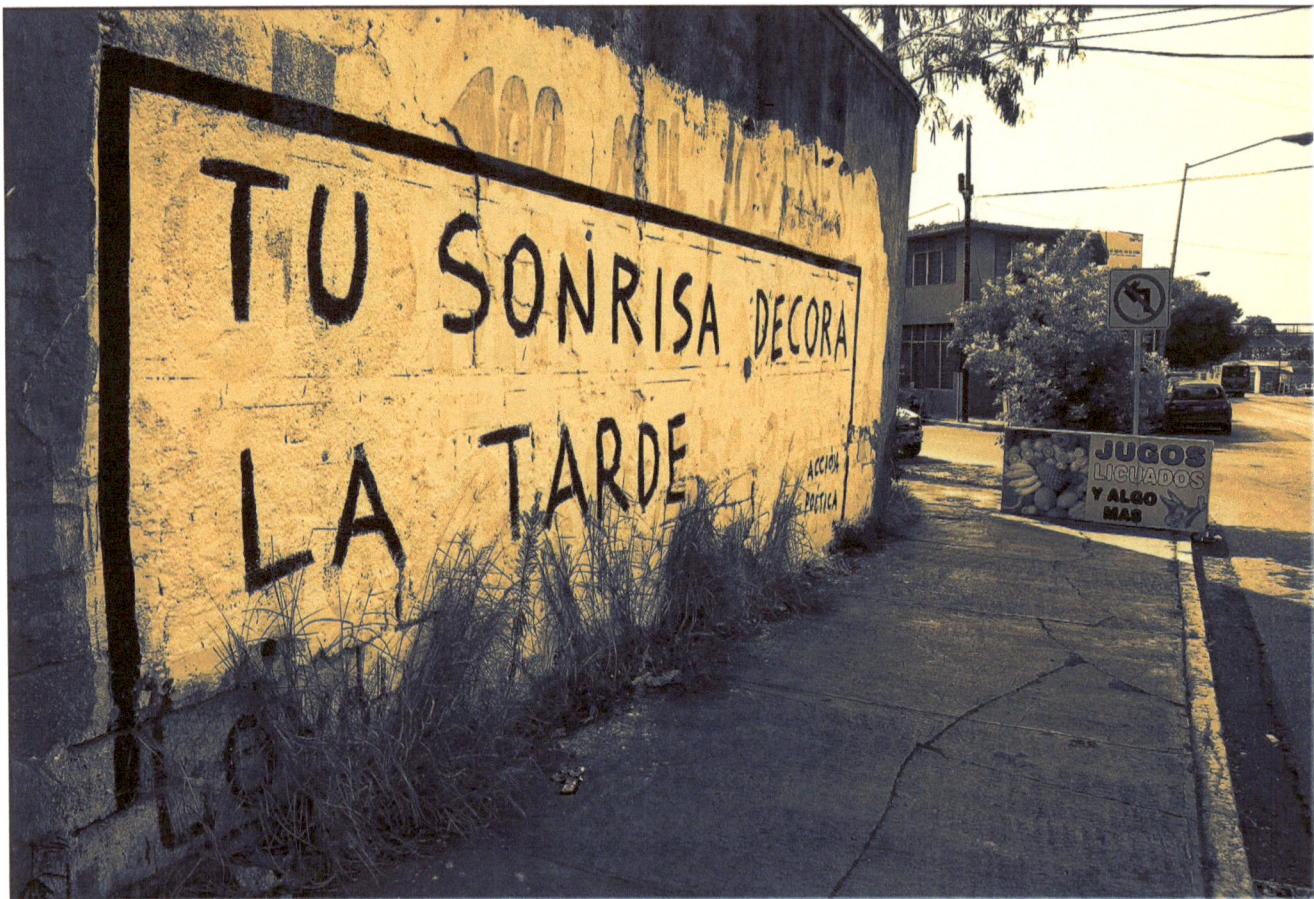

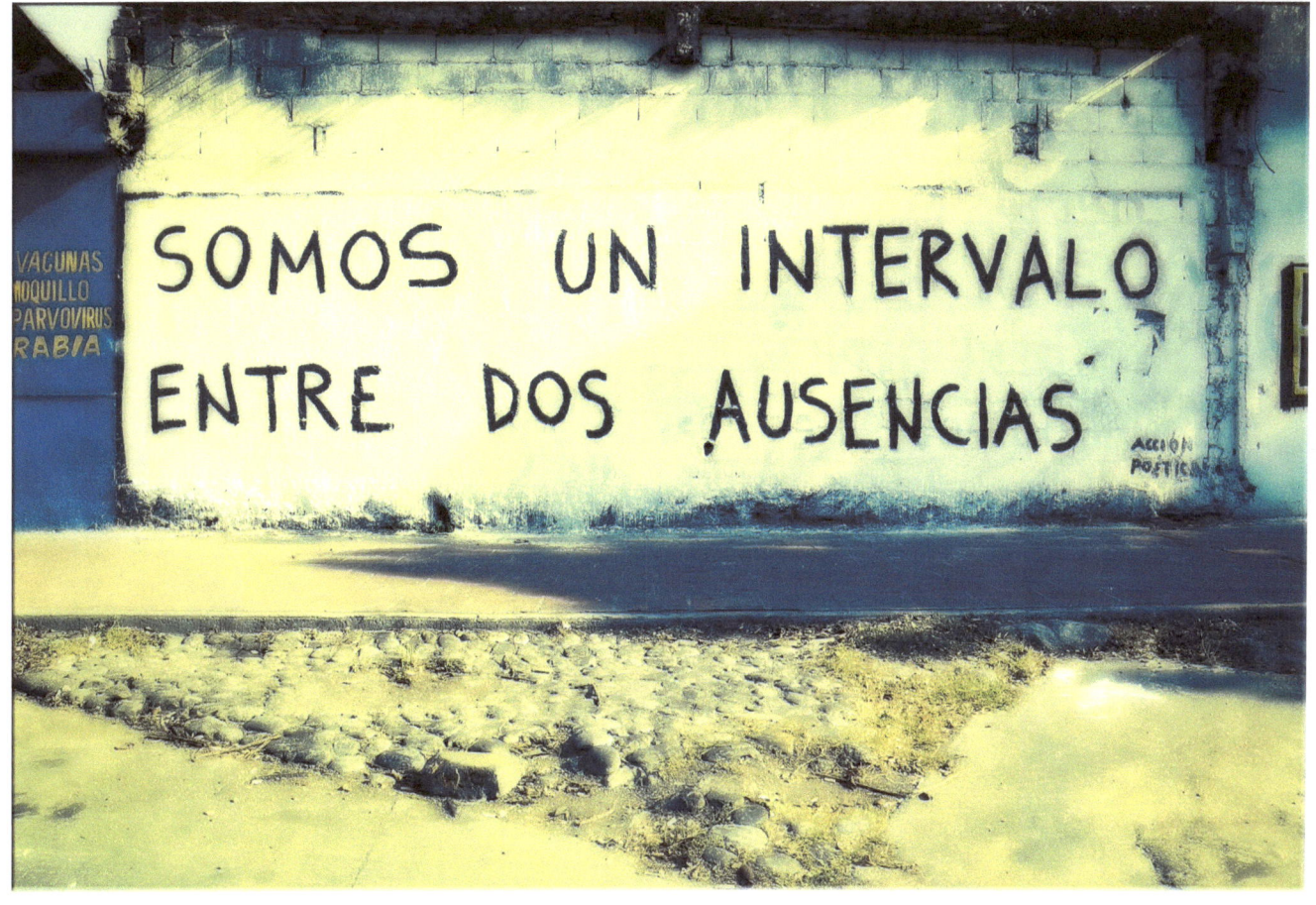

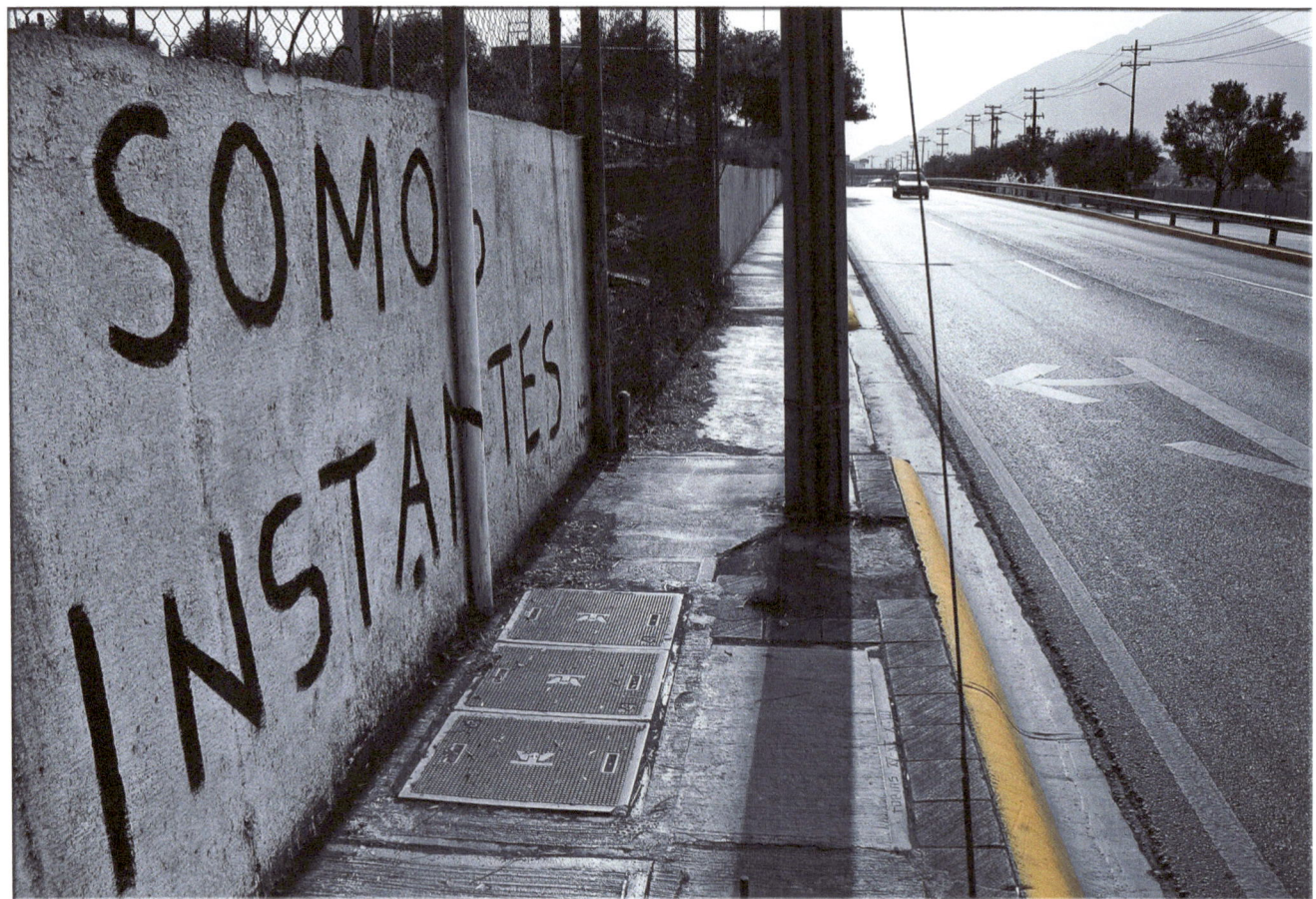

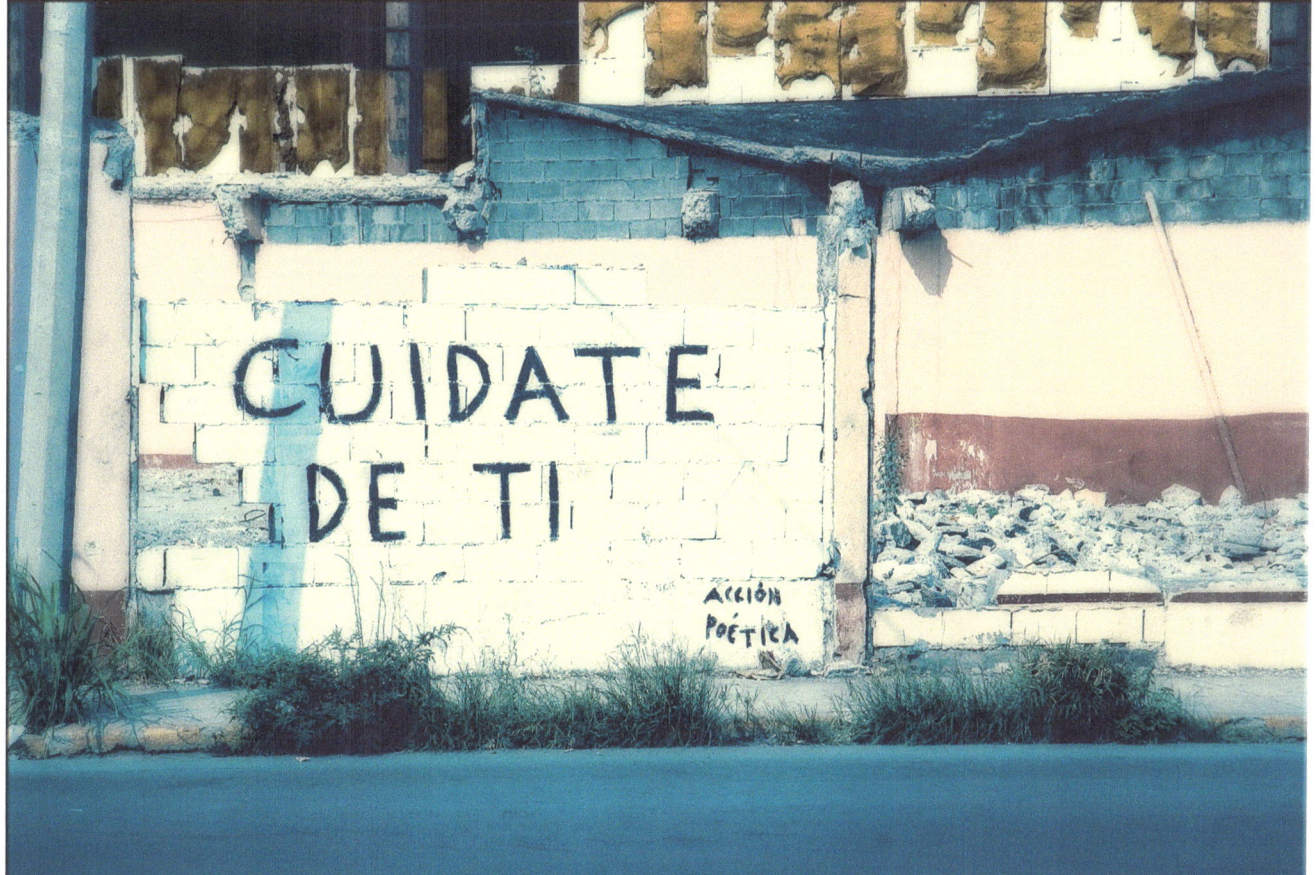

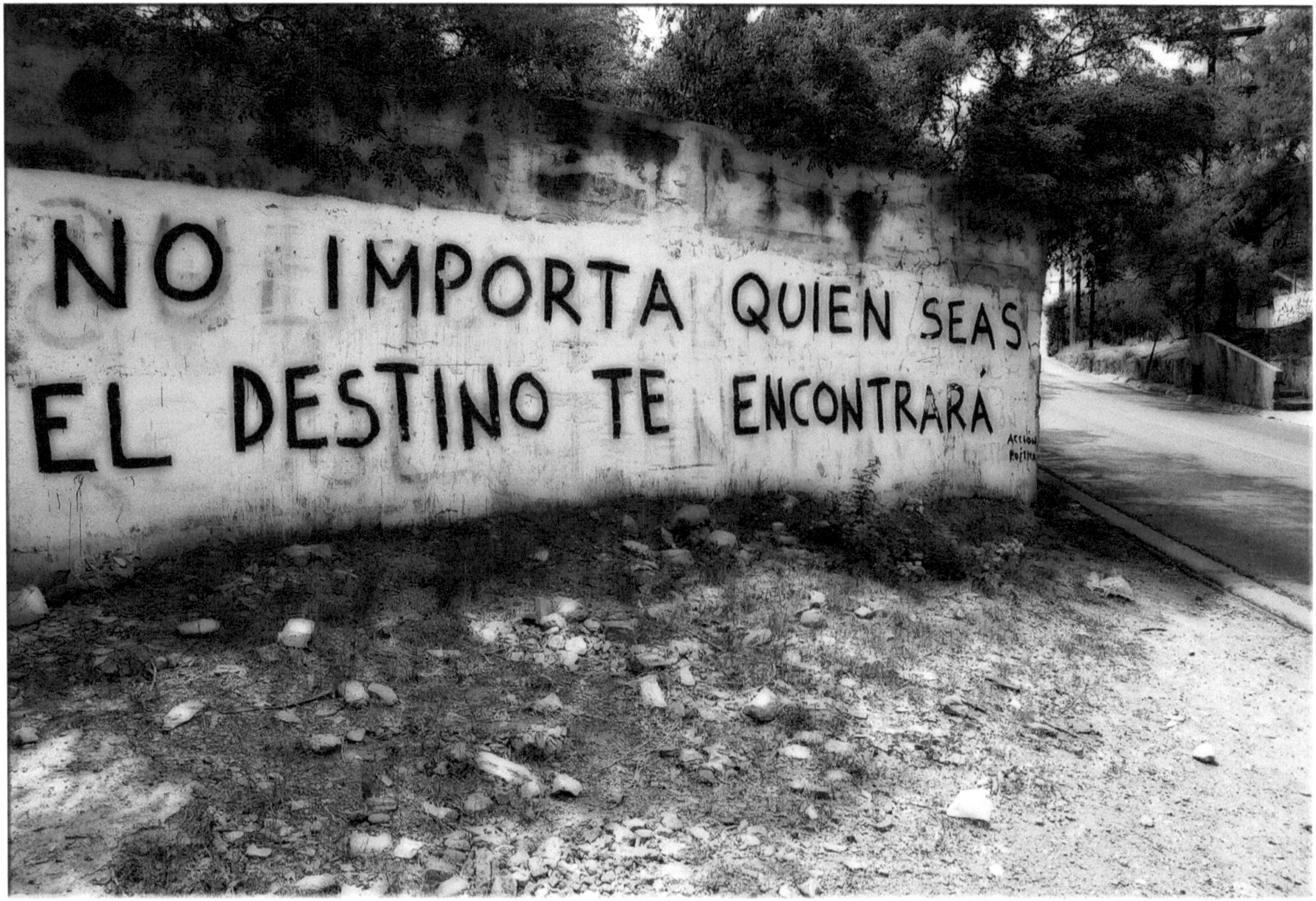
NO IMPORTA QUIEN SEAS
EL DESTINO TE ENCONTRARÁ
Acción

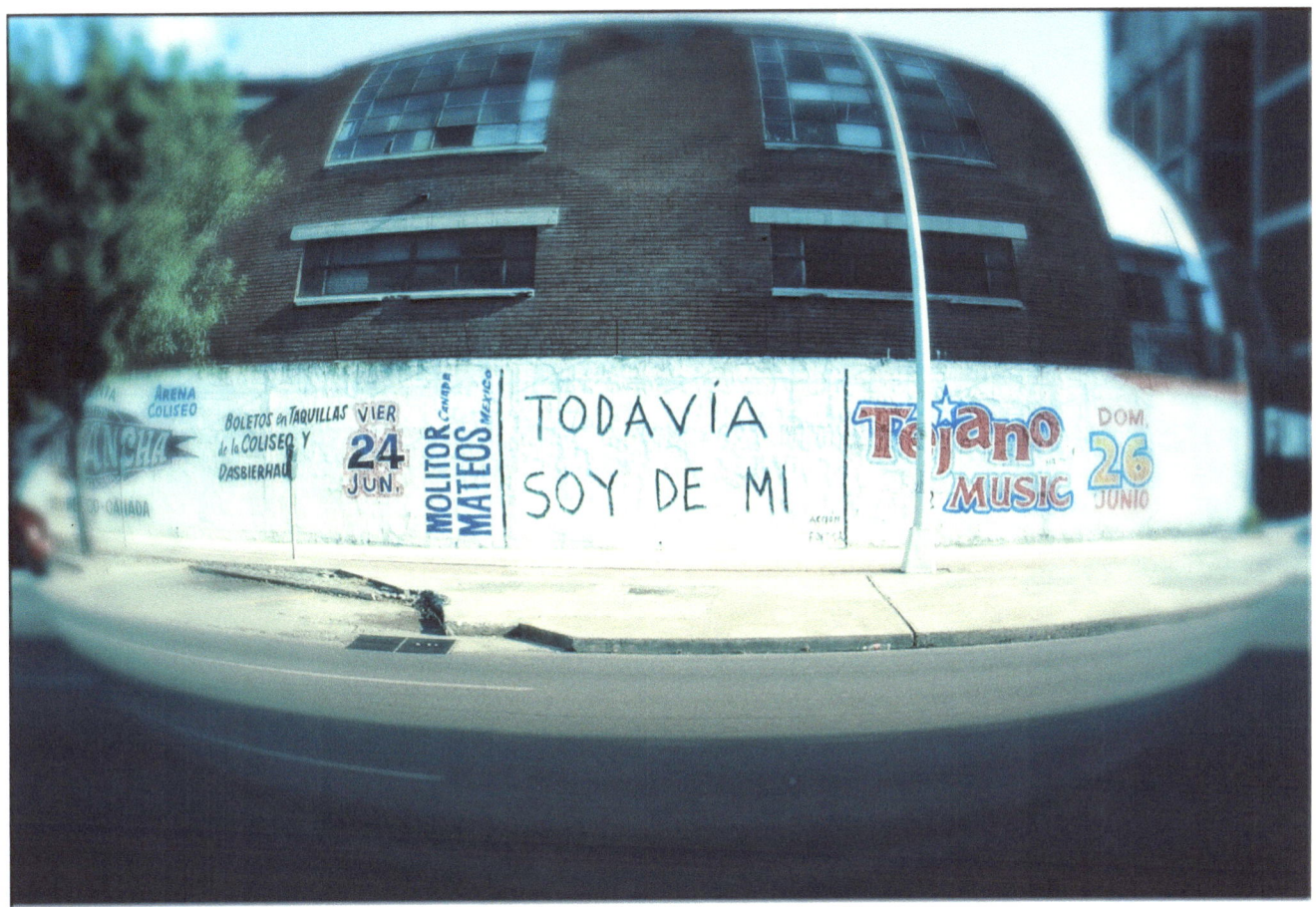

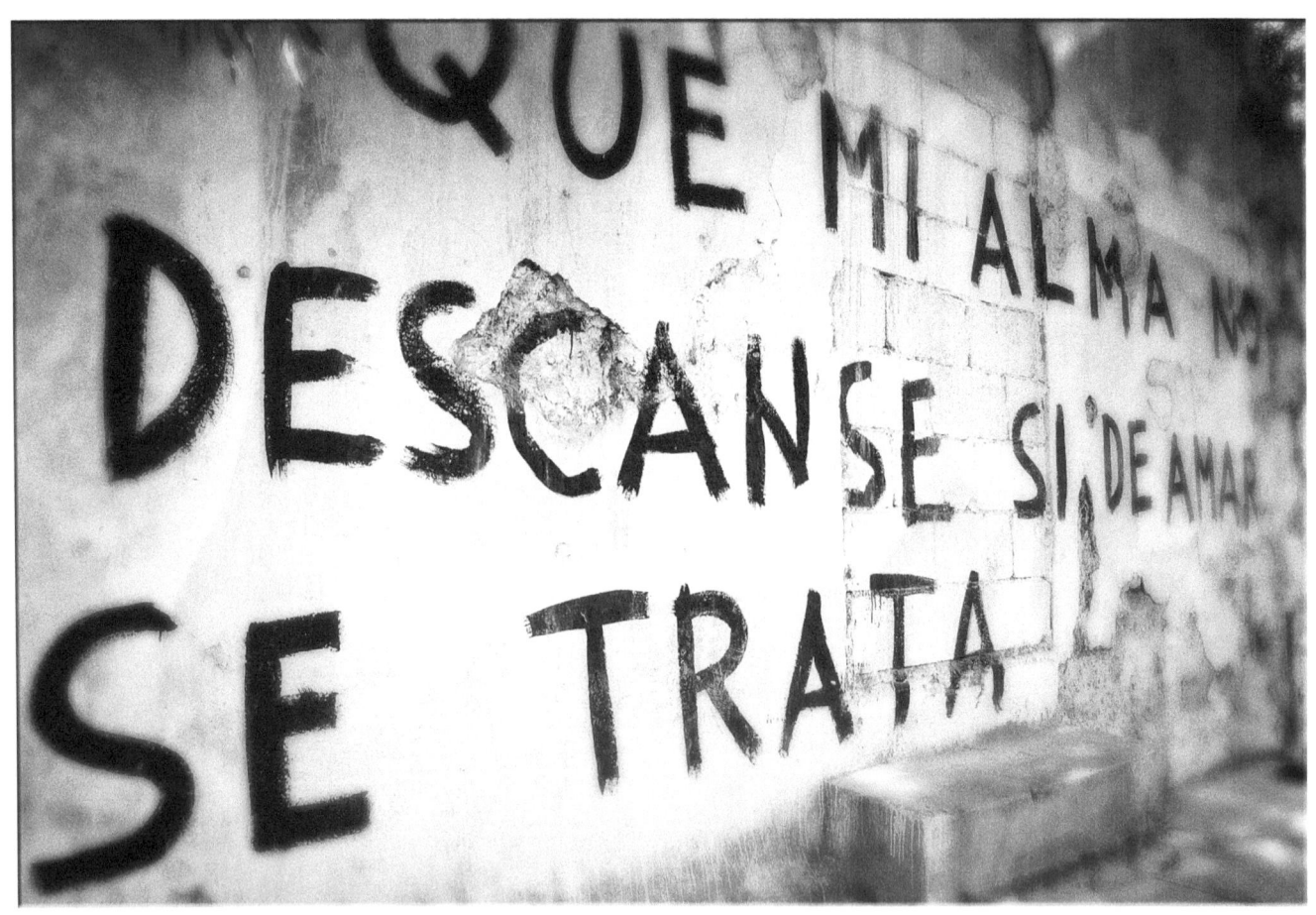

May my soul have no rest, if loving is about

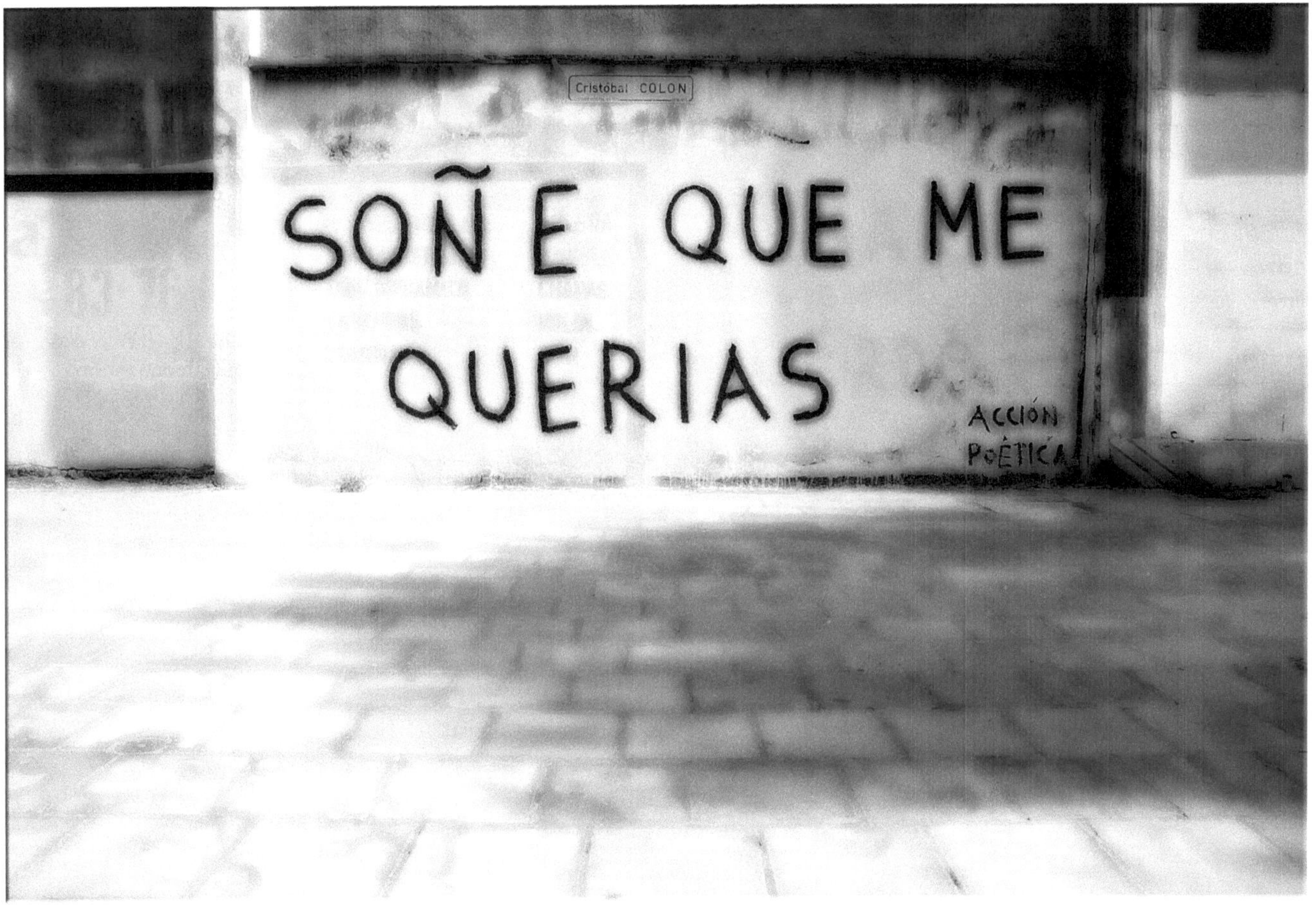
Cristóbal COLON
SOÑE QUE ME
QUERIAS
ACCIÓN
POÉTICA

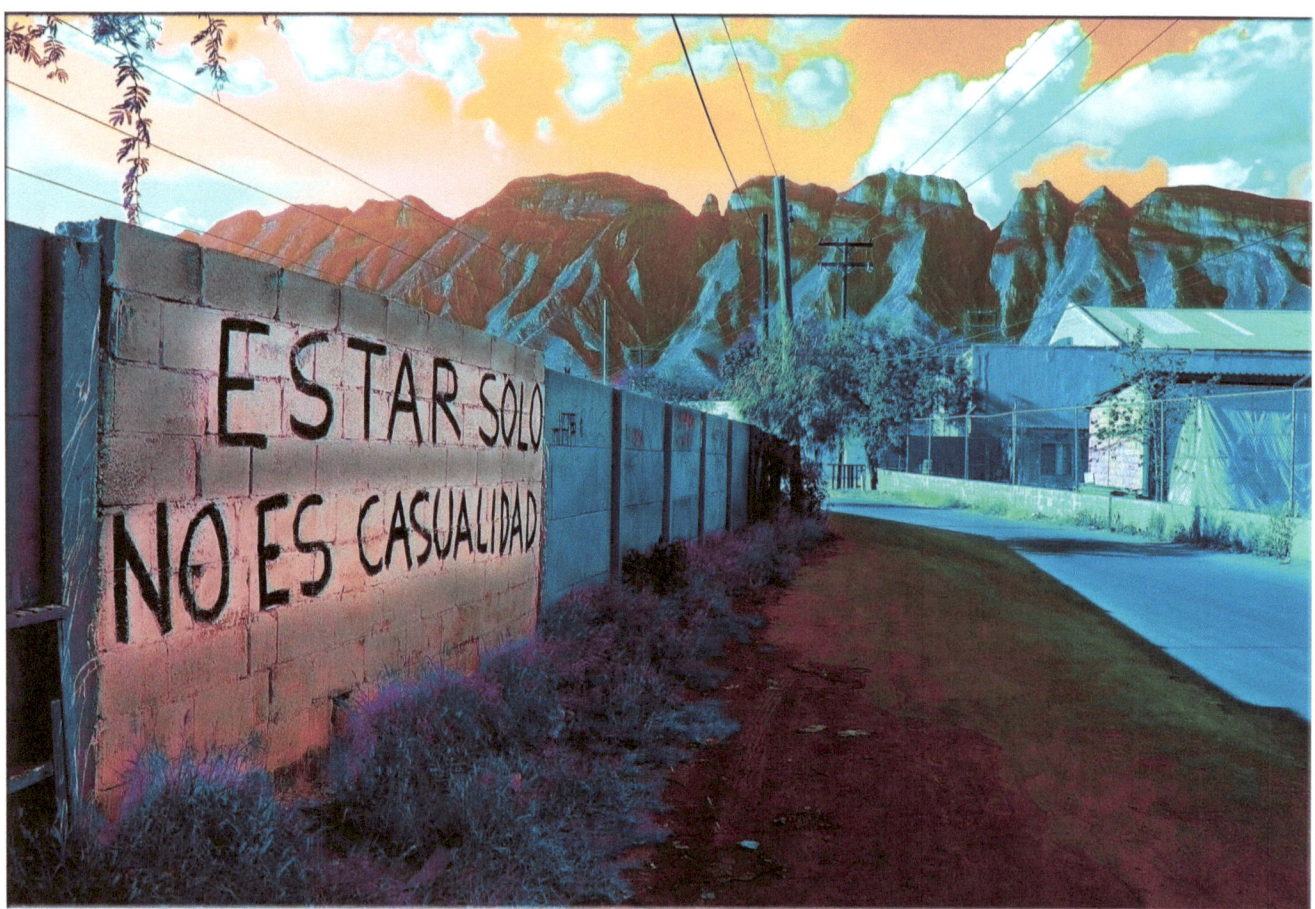

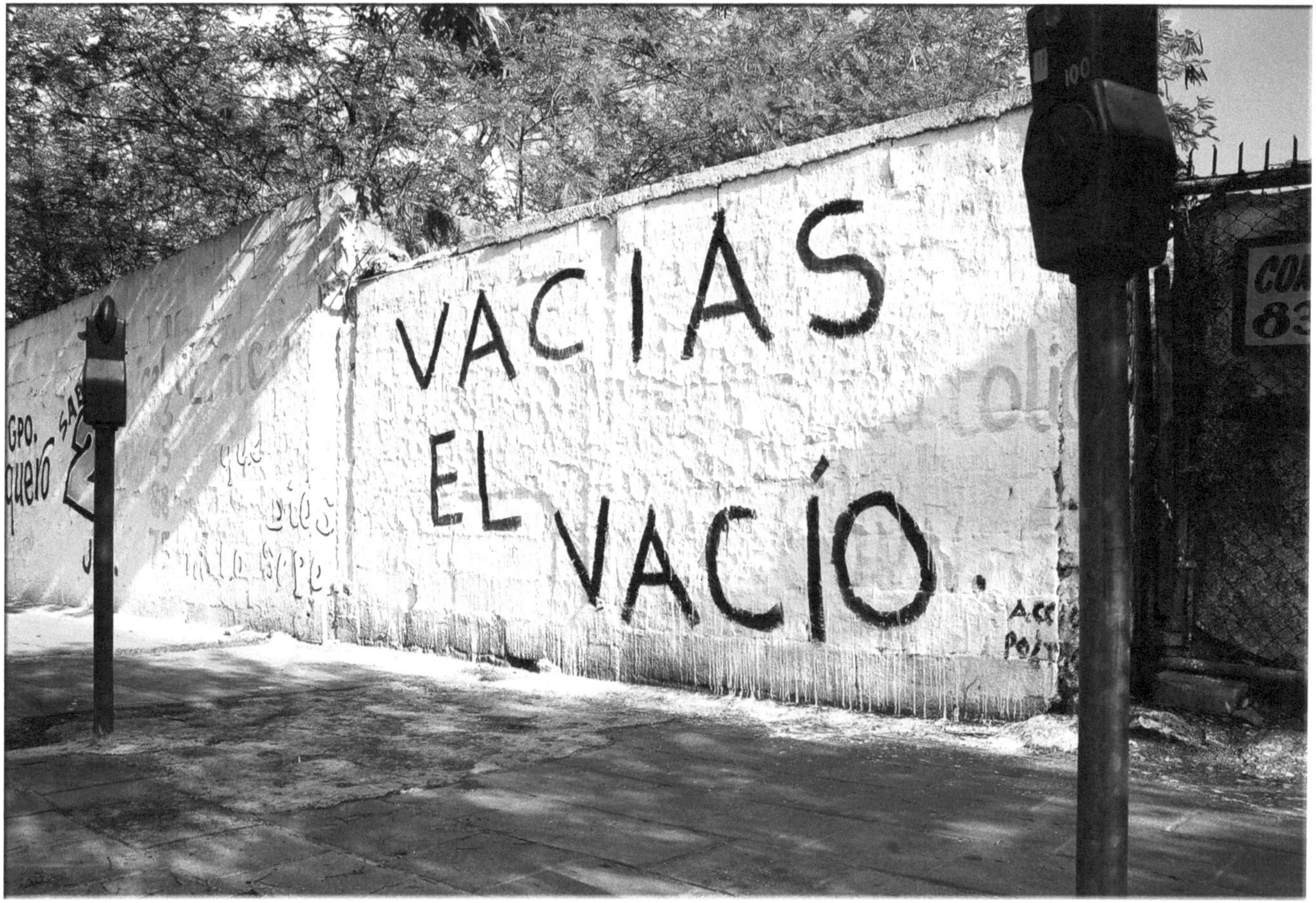
VACIÁS
EL VACÍO.

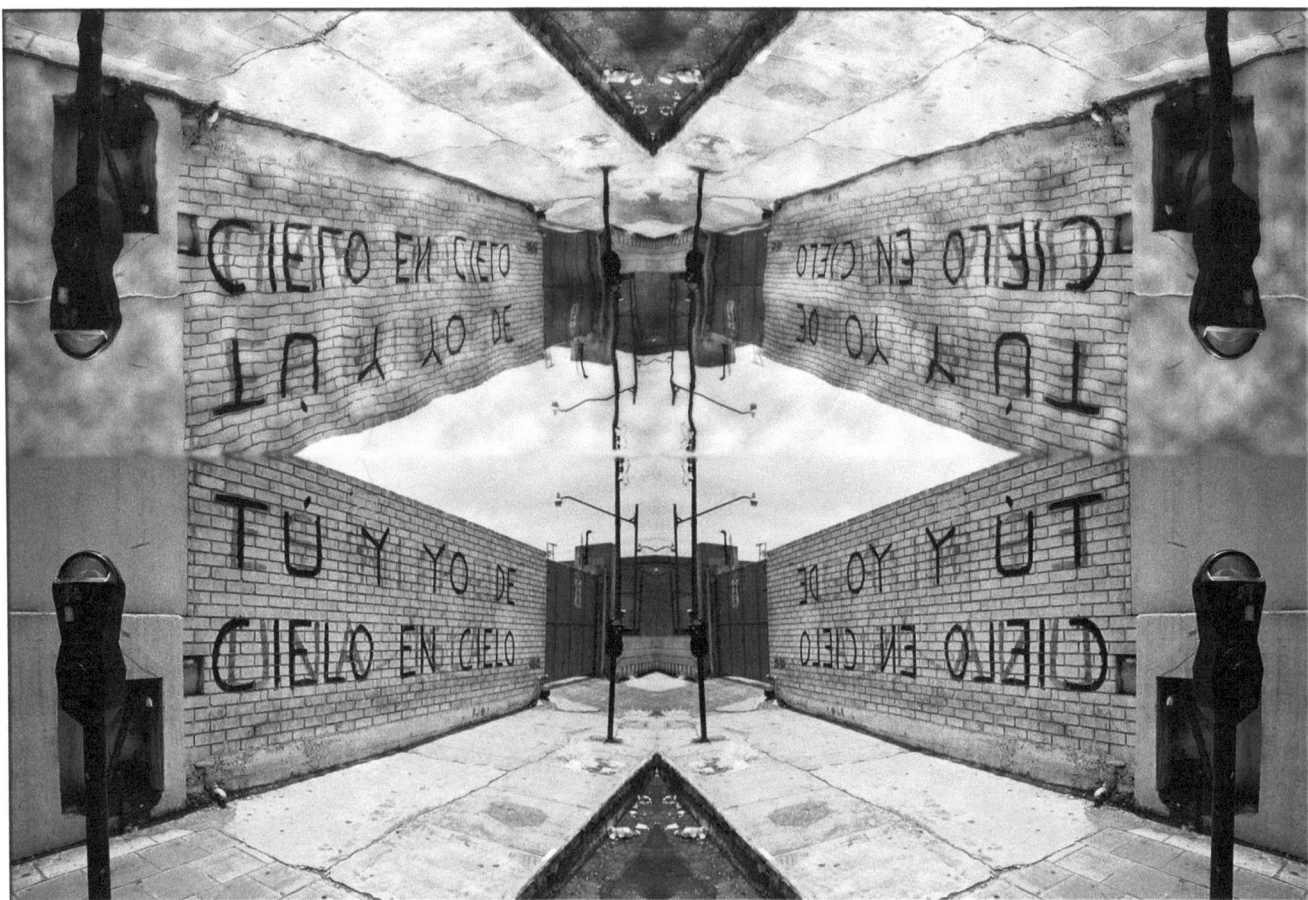

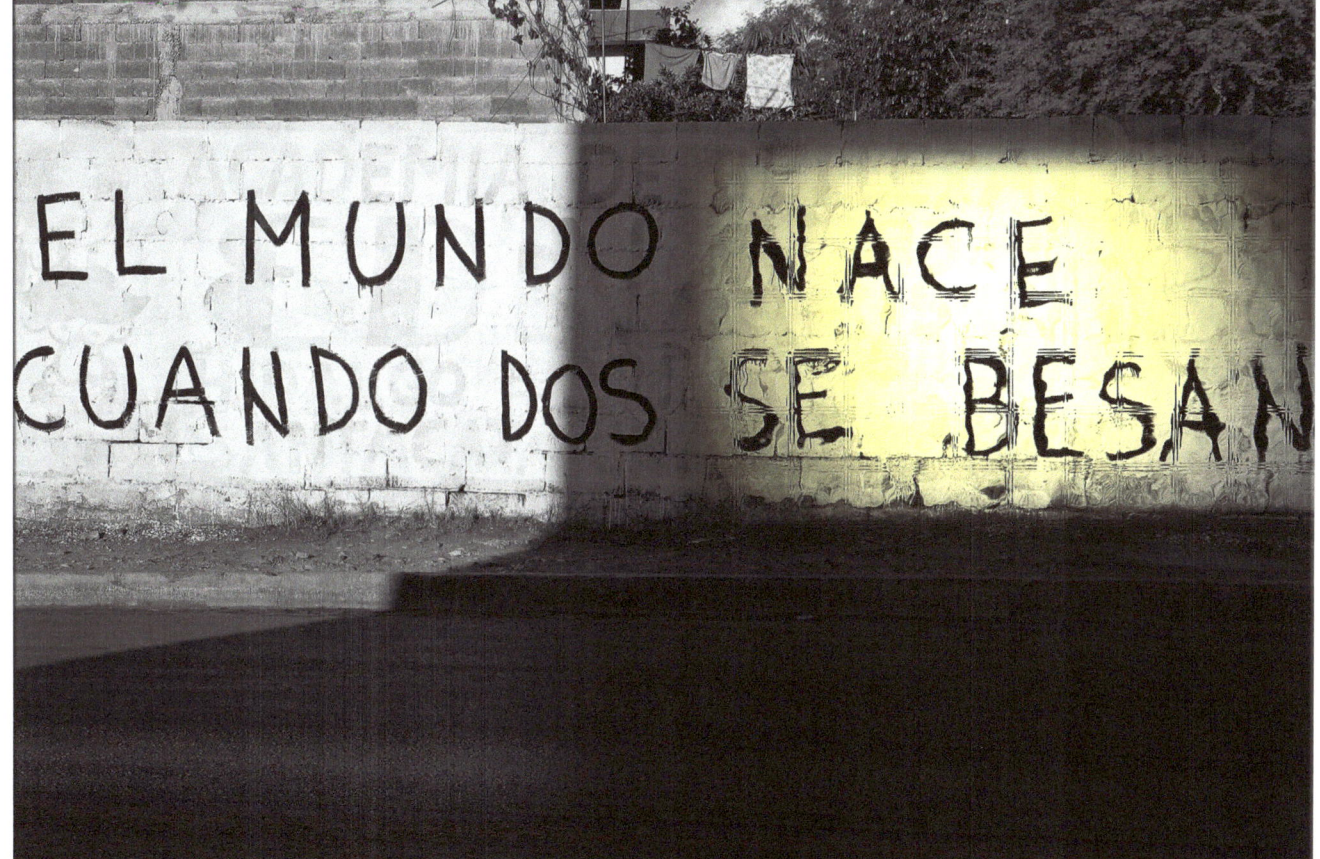

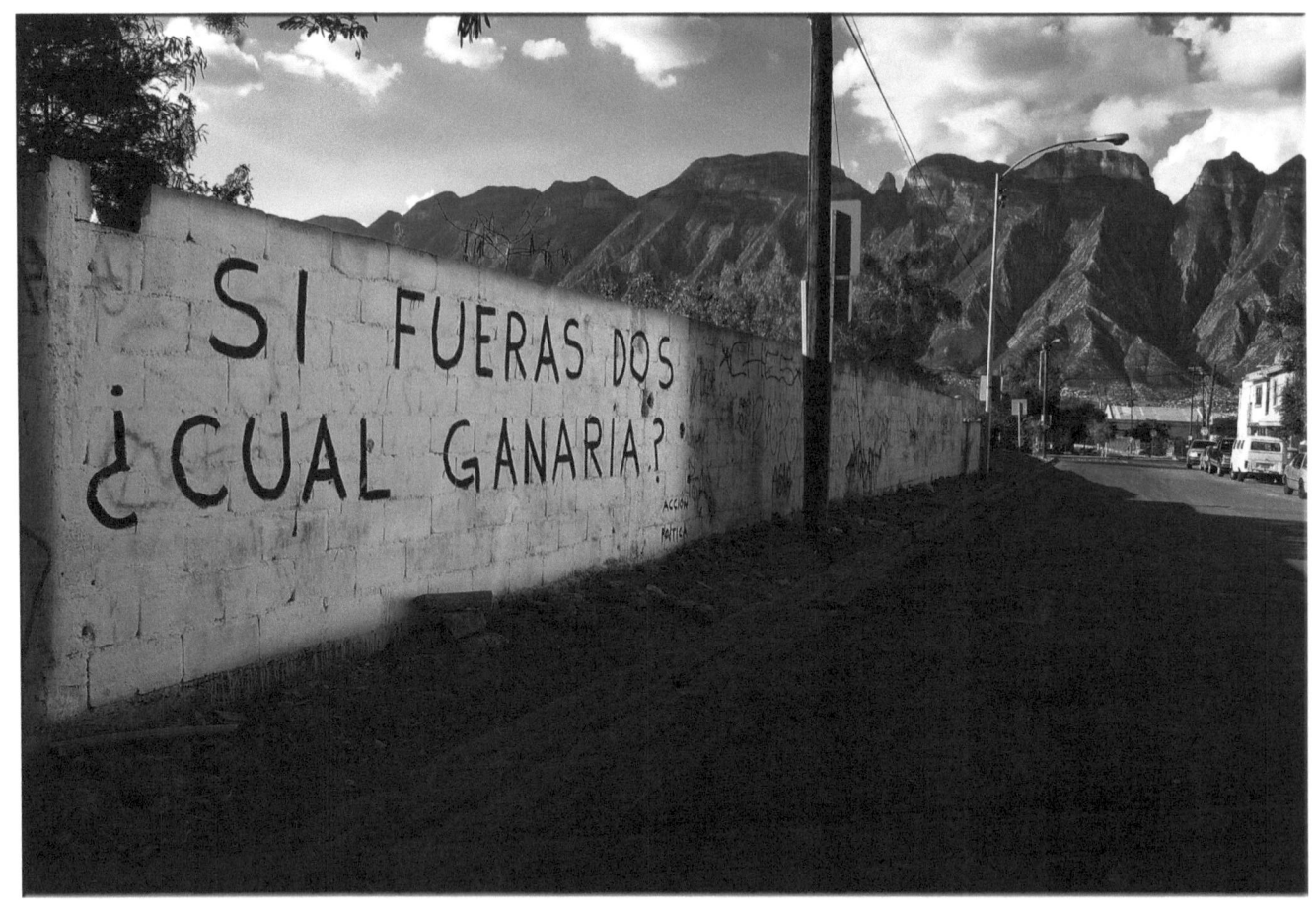

If you were two, which one would win?

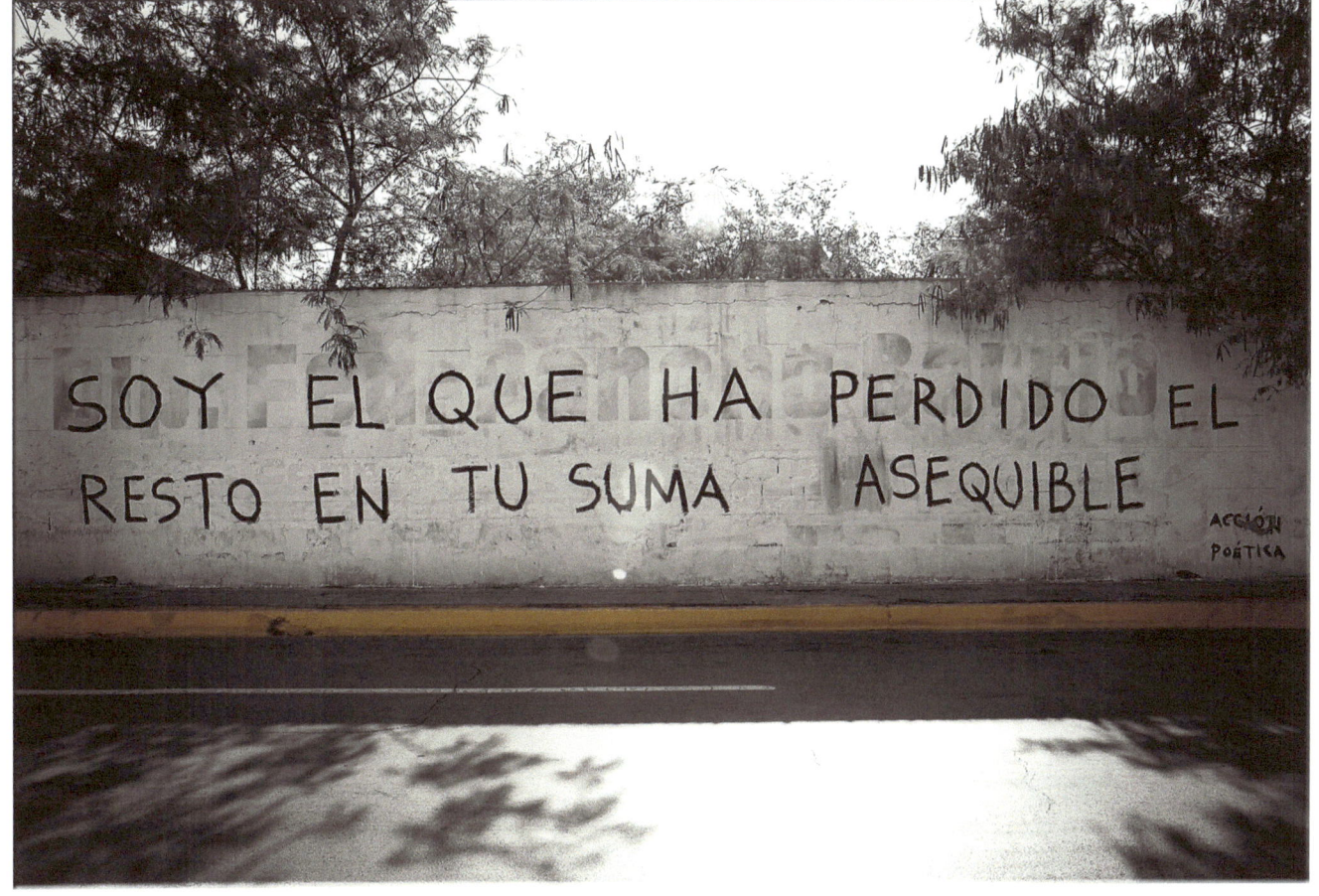

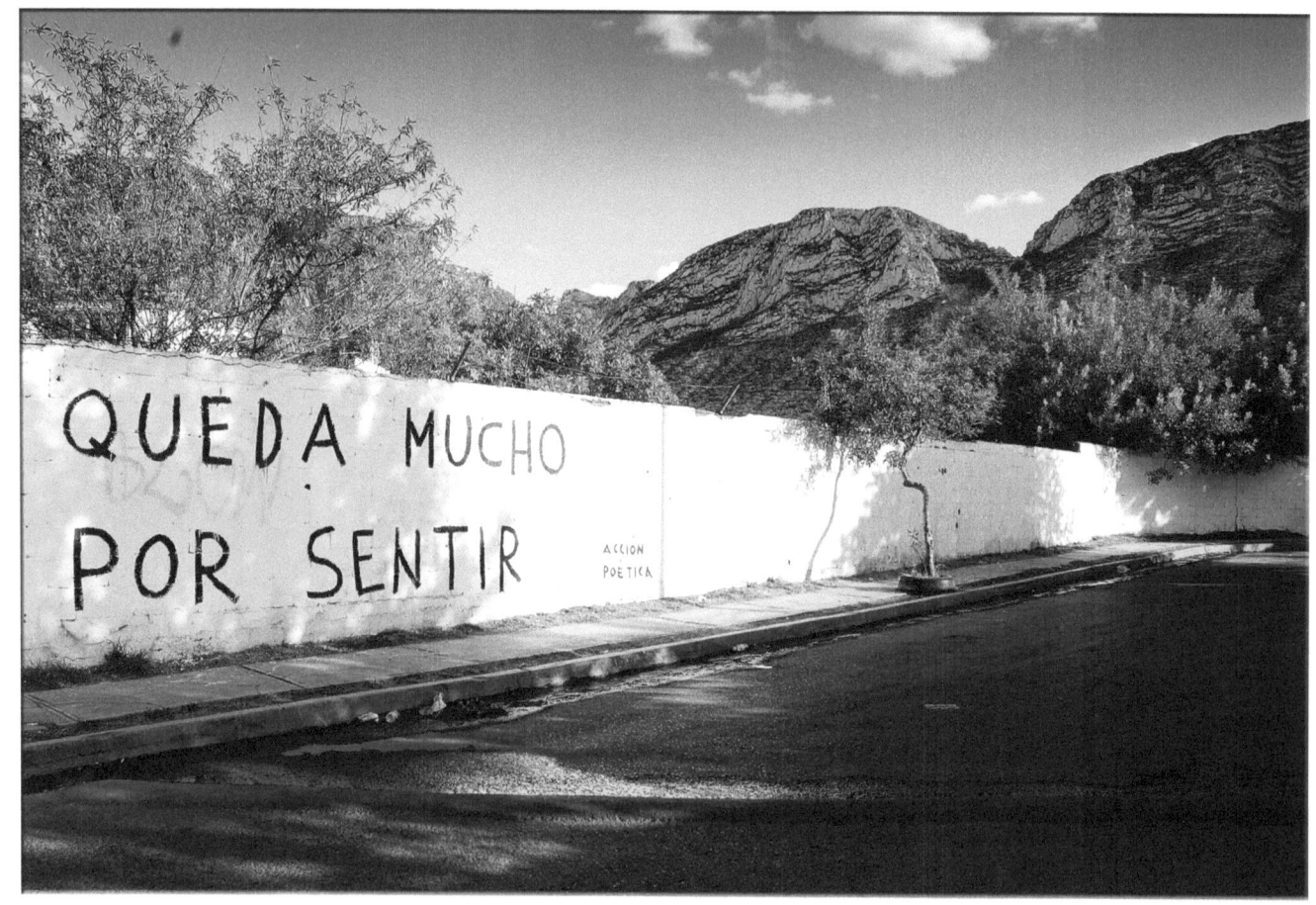

There is still much left to be felt

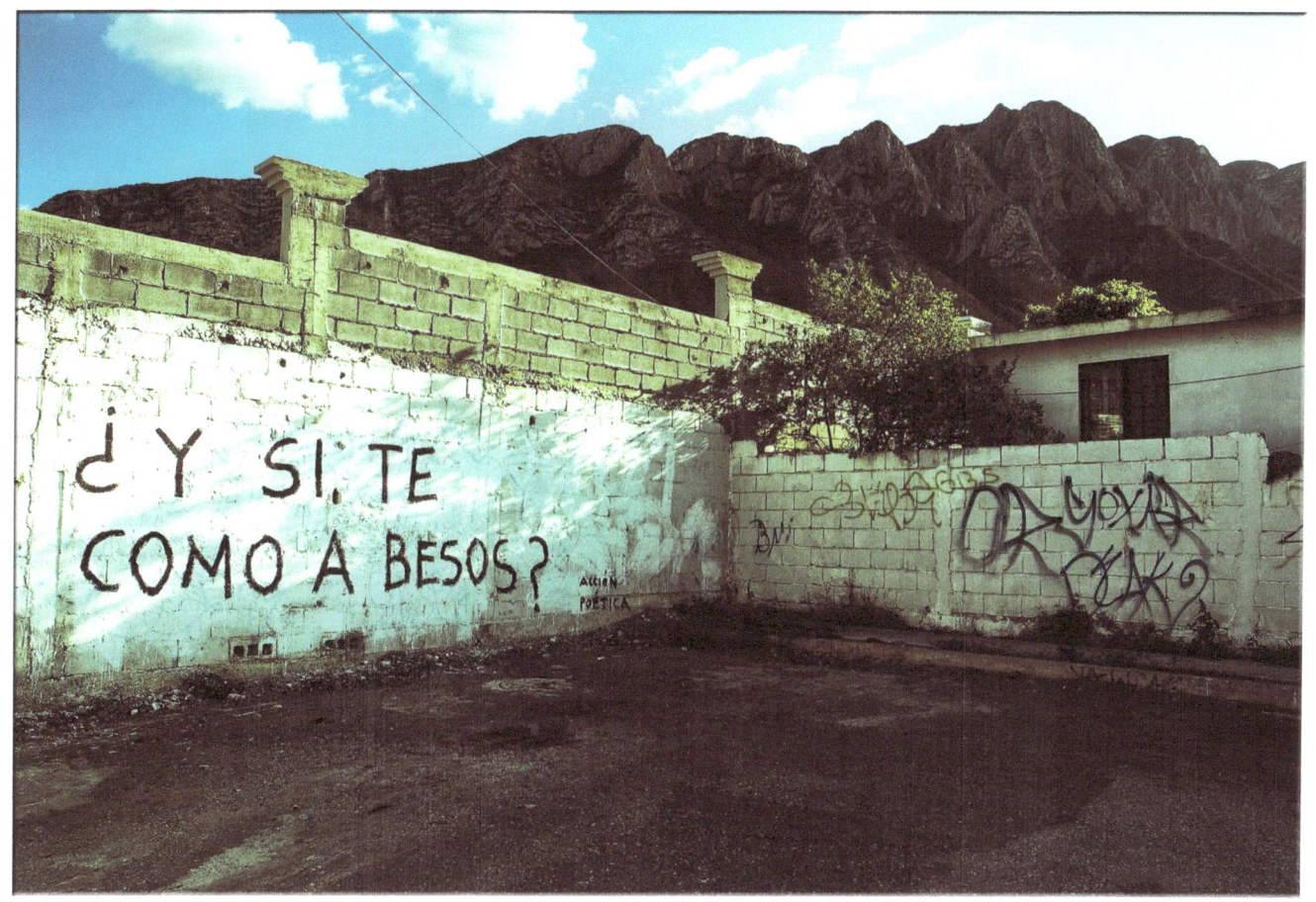

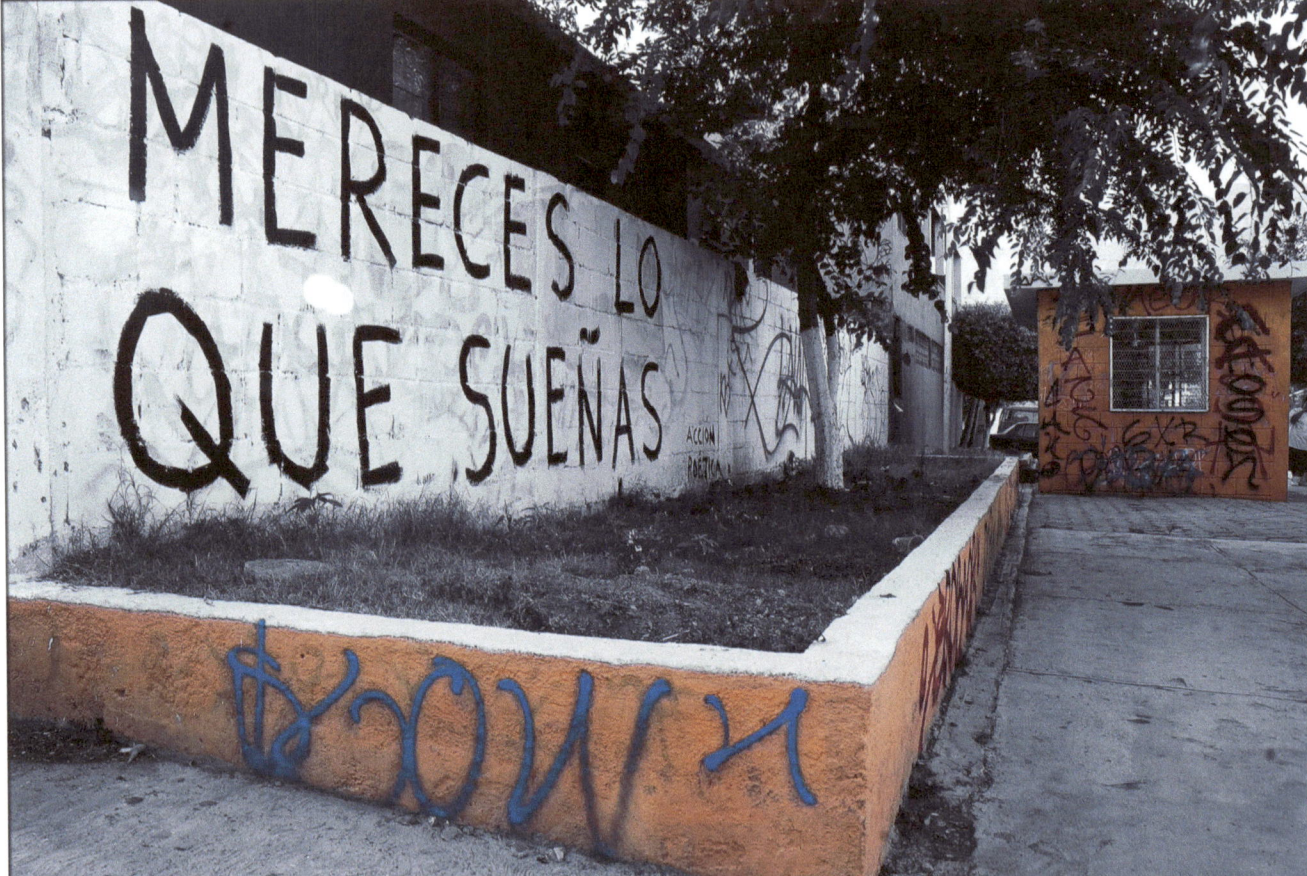

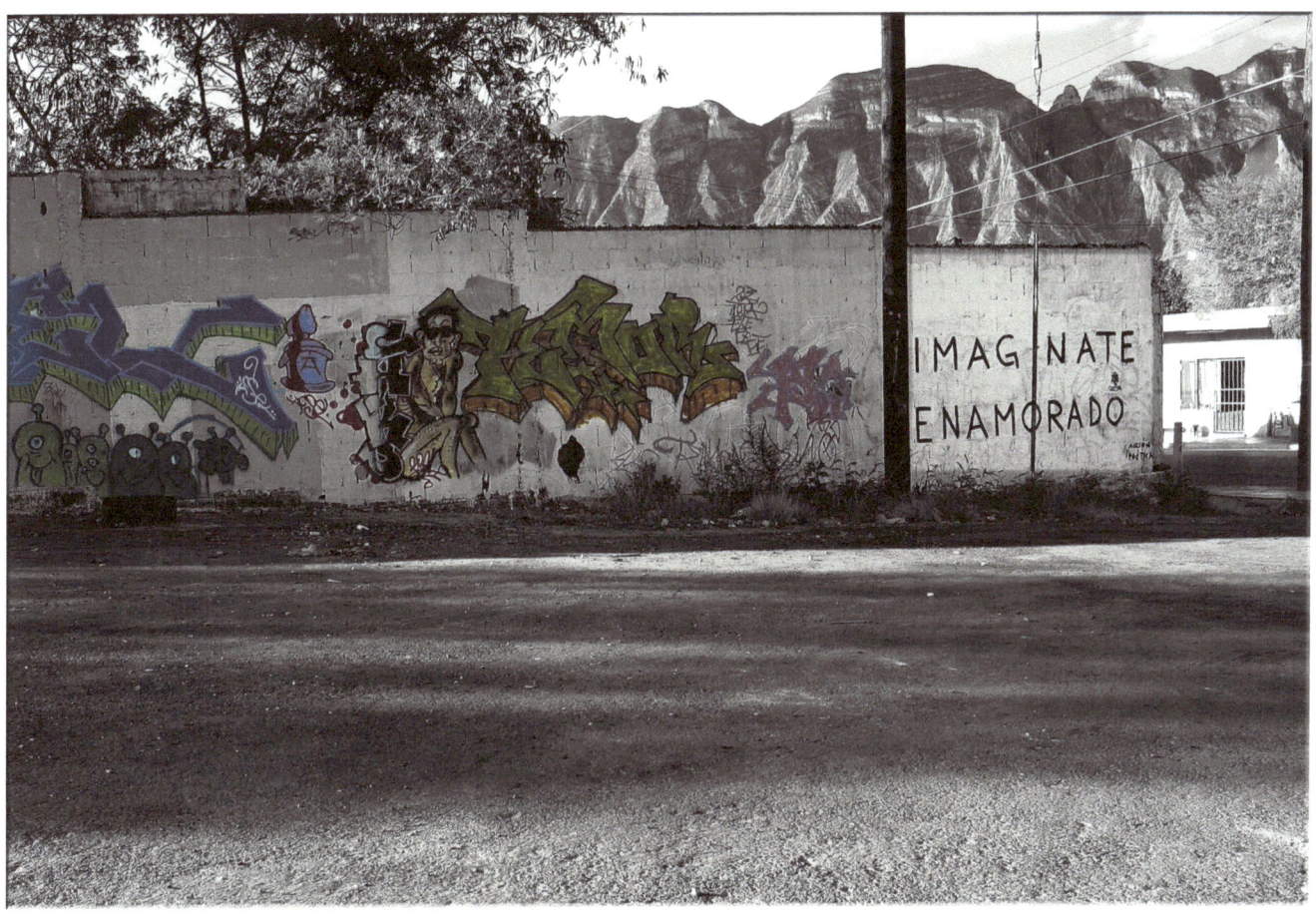

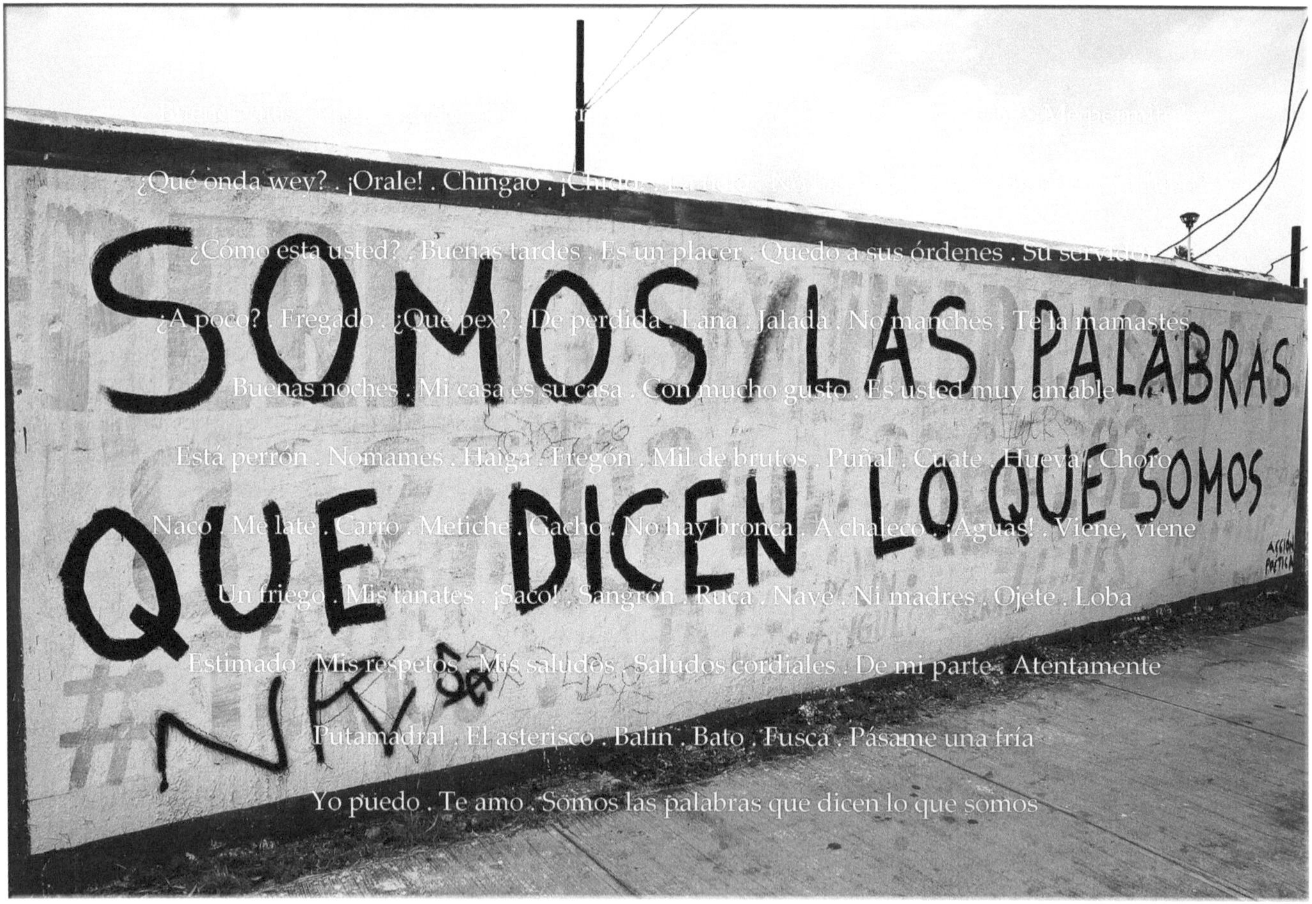
¿Qué onda wey? . ¡Orale! . Chingao .
¿Cómo esta usted? . Buenas tardes . Es un placer . Quedo a sus órdenes . Su servidor
¿A poco? . Fregado . ¿Qué pex? . De perdida . Lana . Jalada . No manches . Te la mamastes
Buenas noches . Mi casa es su casa . Con mucho gusto . Es usted muy amable
Está perrón . Nomames . Haiga . Fregón . Mil de brutos . Puñal . Cuate . Hueva . Choro
Naco . Me late . Carro . Metiche . Gacho . No hay bronca . A chaleco . ¡Aguas! . Viene, viene
Un friego . Mis tanates . ¡Saco! . Sangrón . Ruca . Nave . Ni madres . Ojete . Loba
Estimado . Mis respetos . Mis saludos . Saludos cordiales . De mi parte . Atentamente
Putamadral . El asterisco . Balín . Bato . Fusca . Pásame una fría
Yo puedo . Te amo . Somos las palabras que dicen lo que somos
SOMOS LAS PALABRAS
QUE DICEN LO QUE SOMOS
ACCIÓN POÉTICA

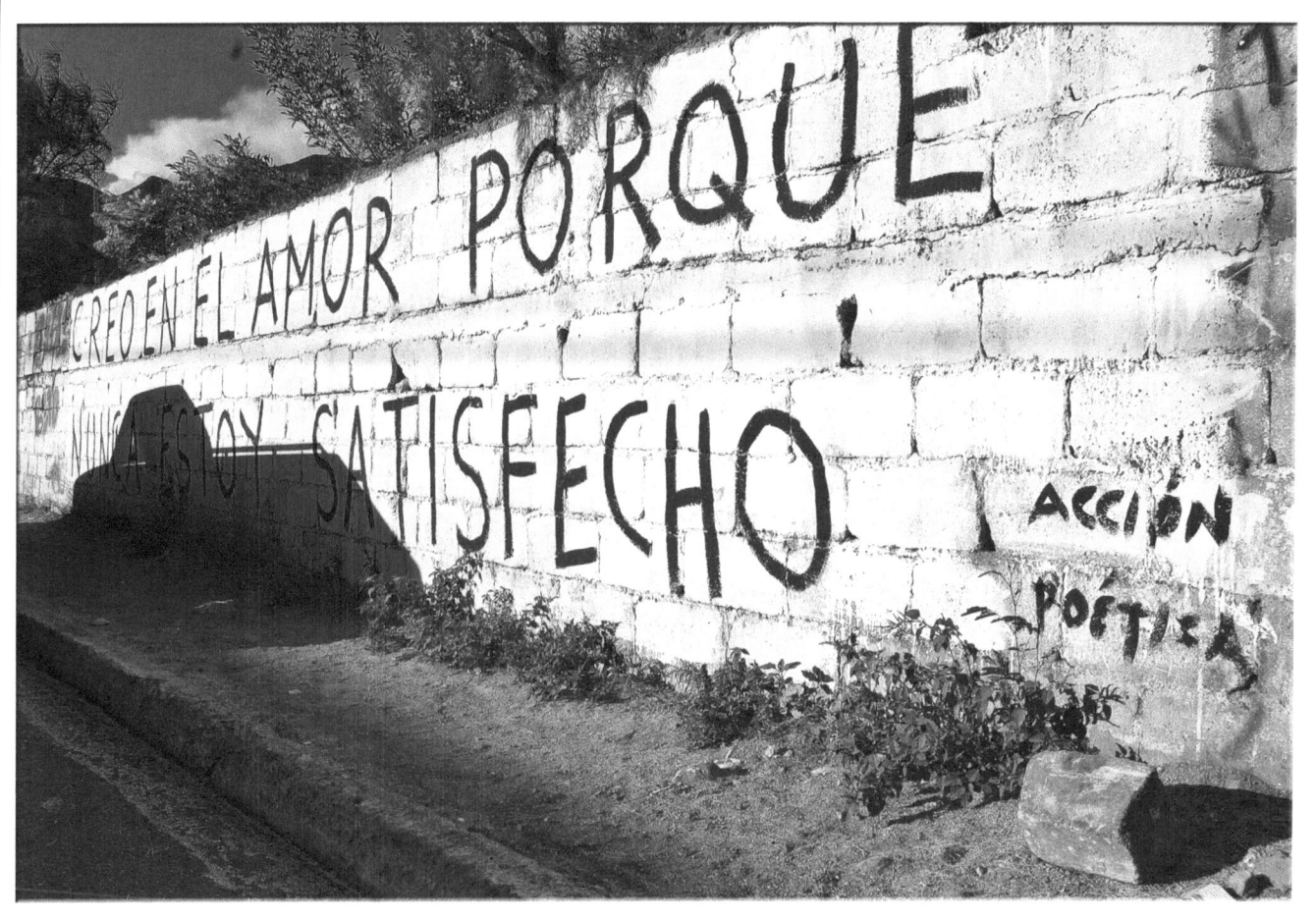

I believe in love because I am never satisfied

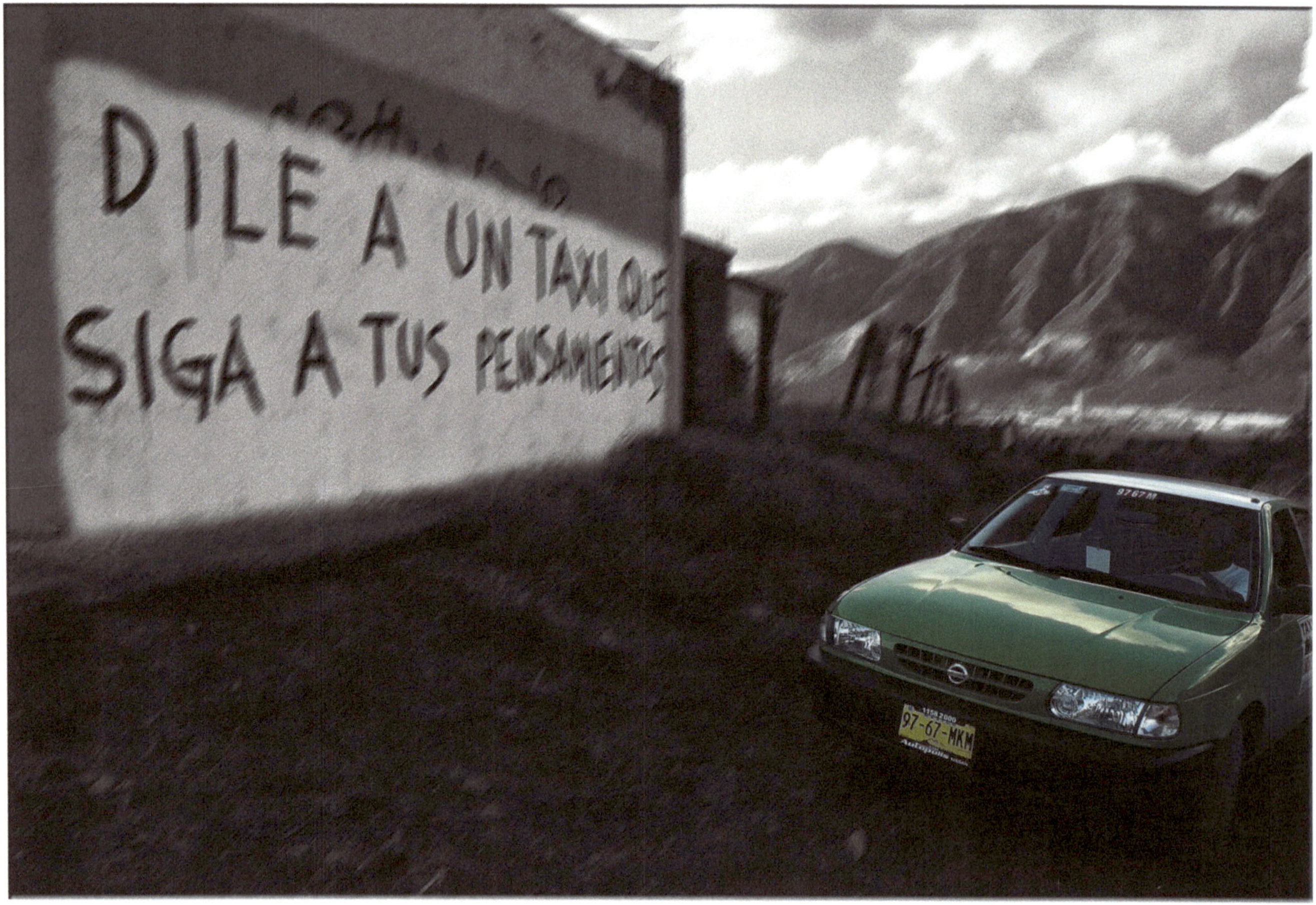
DILE A UN TAXI QUE
SIGA A TUS PENSAMIENTOS
97-67-MKM

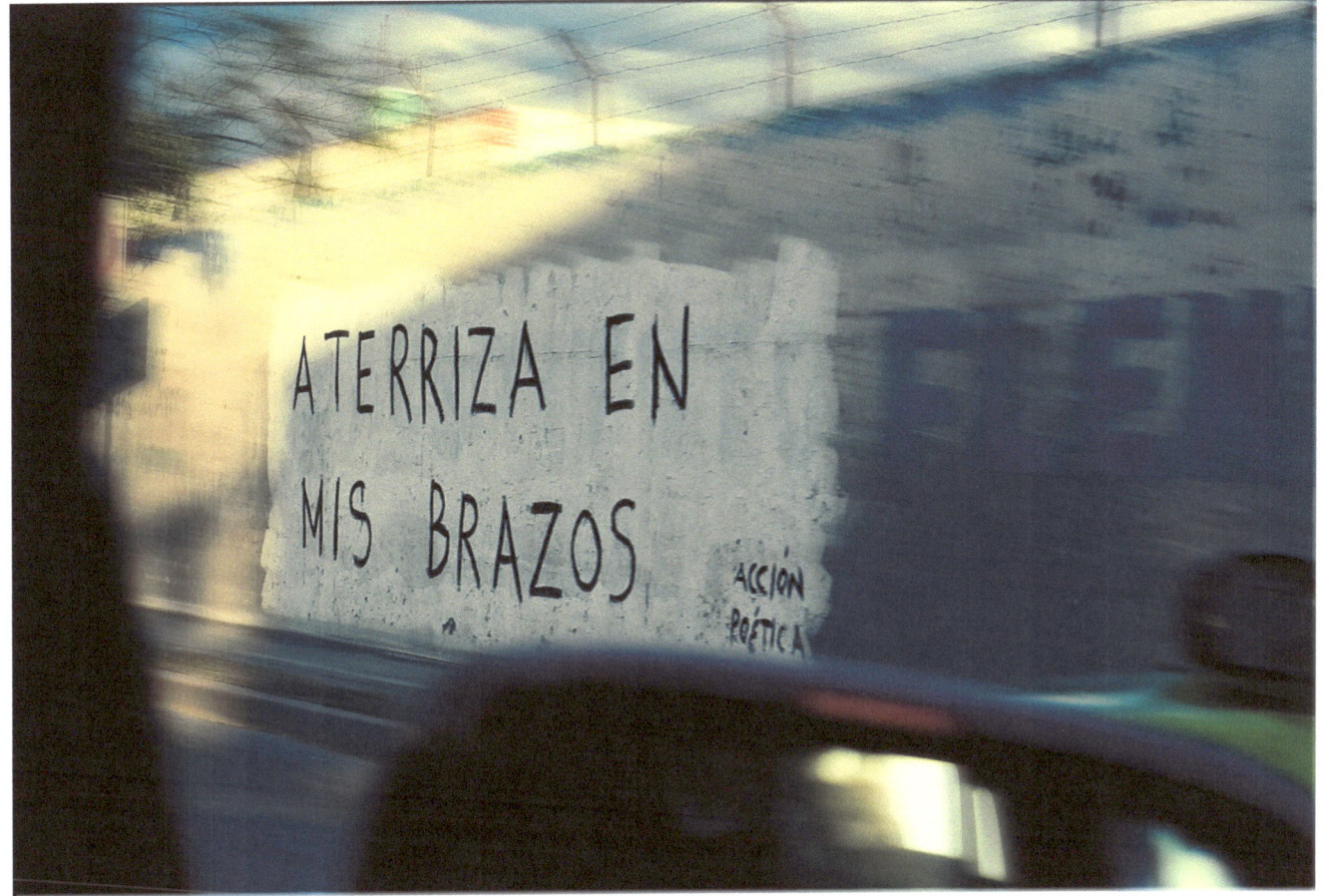

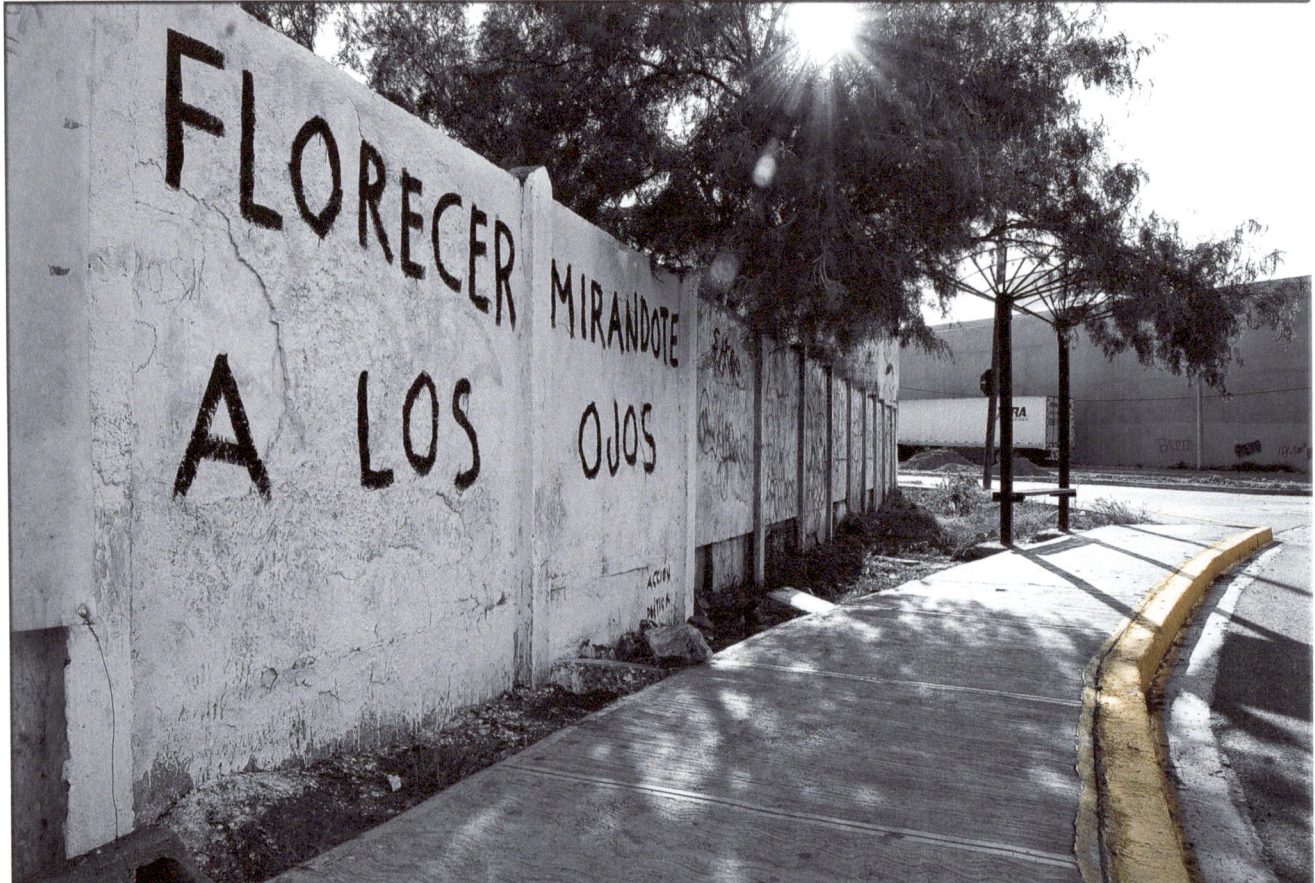

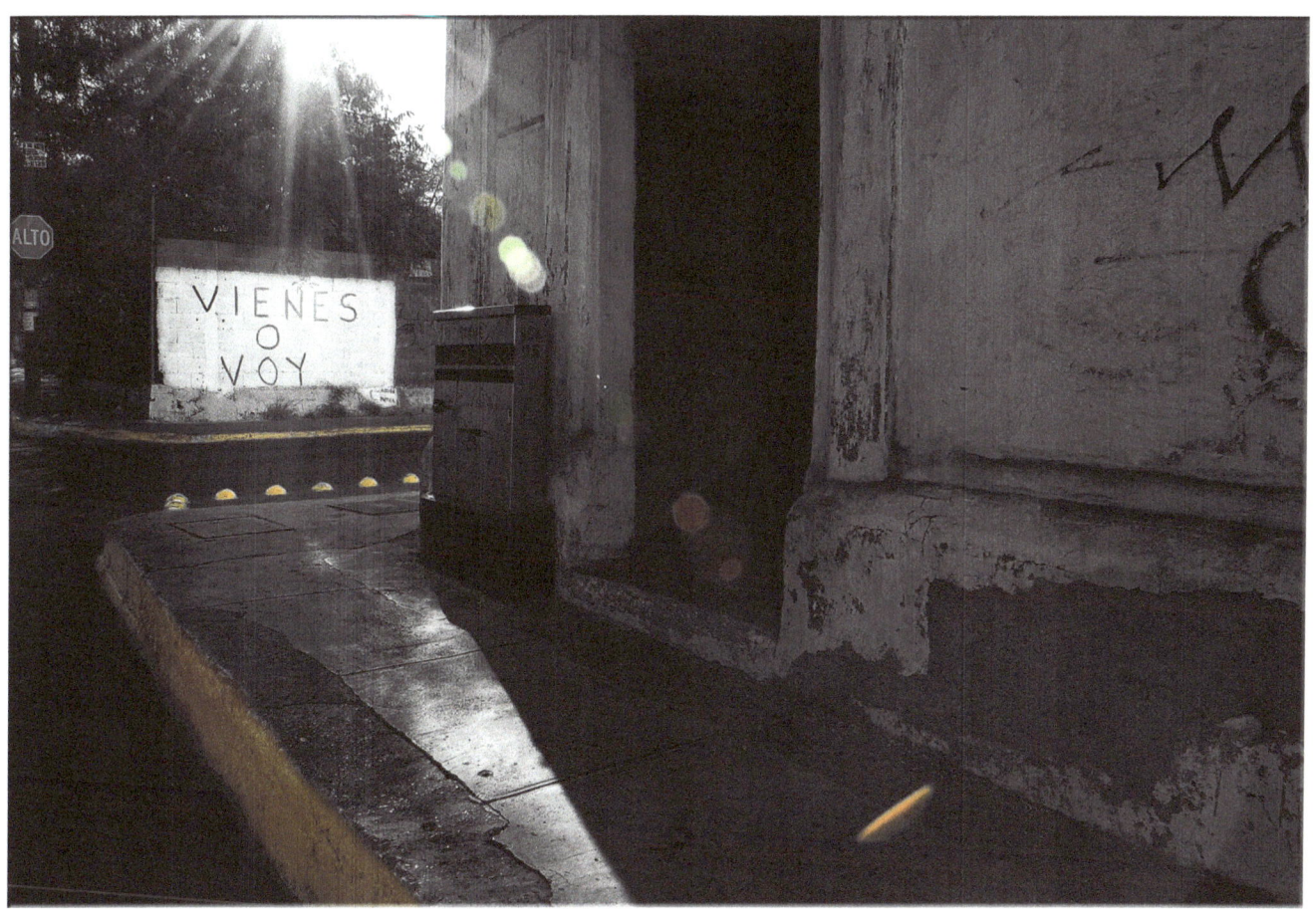

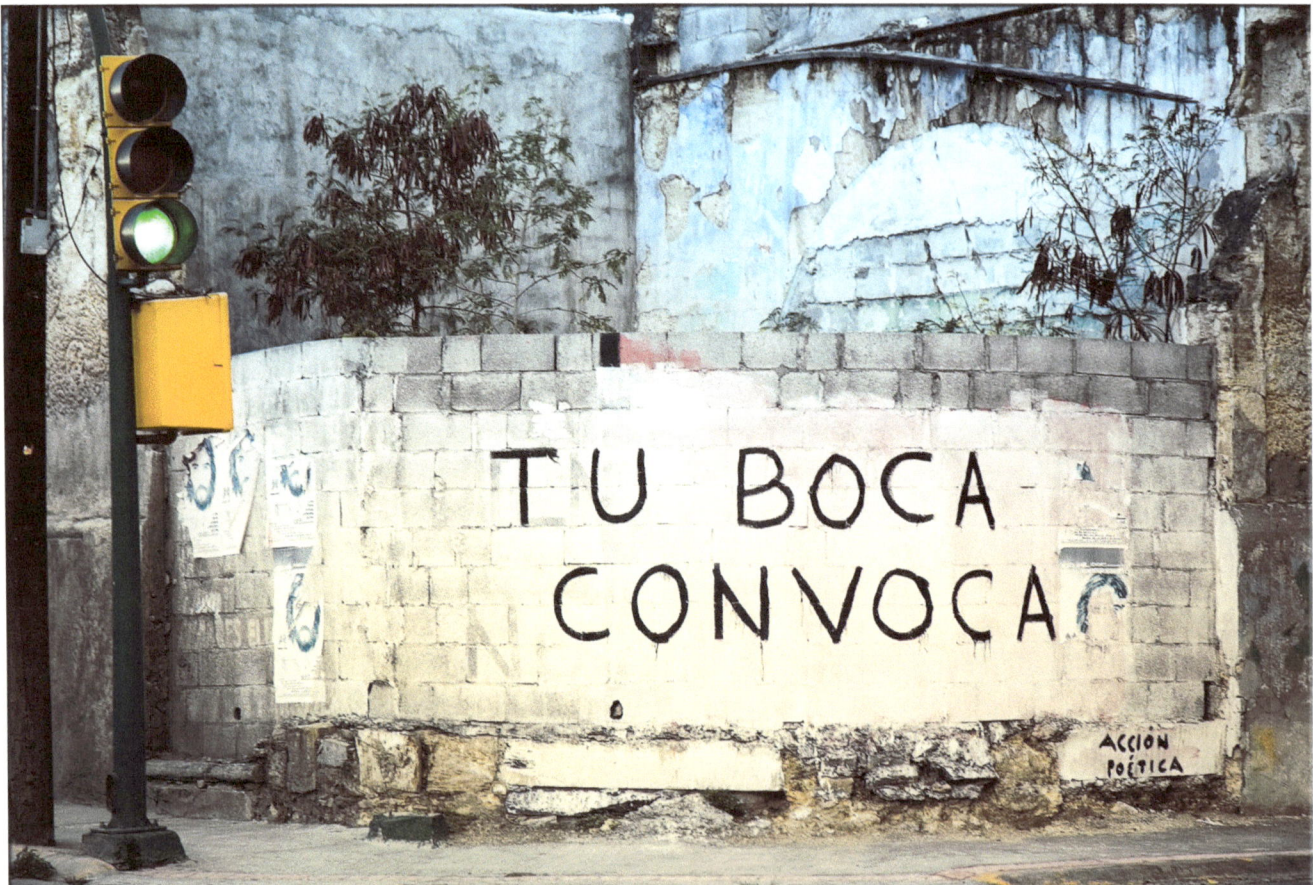

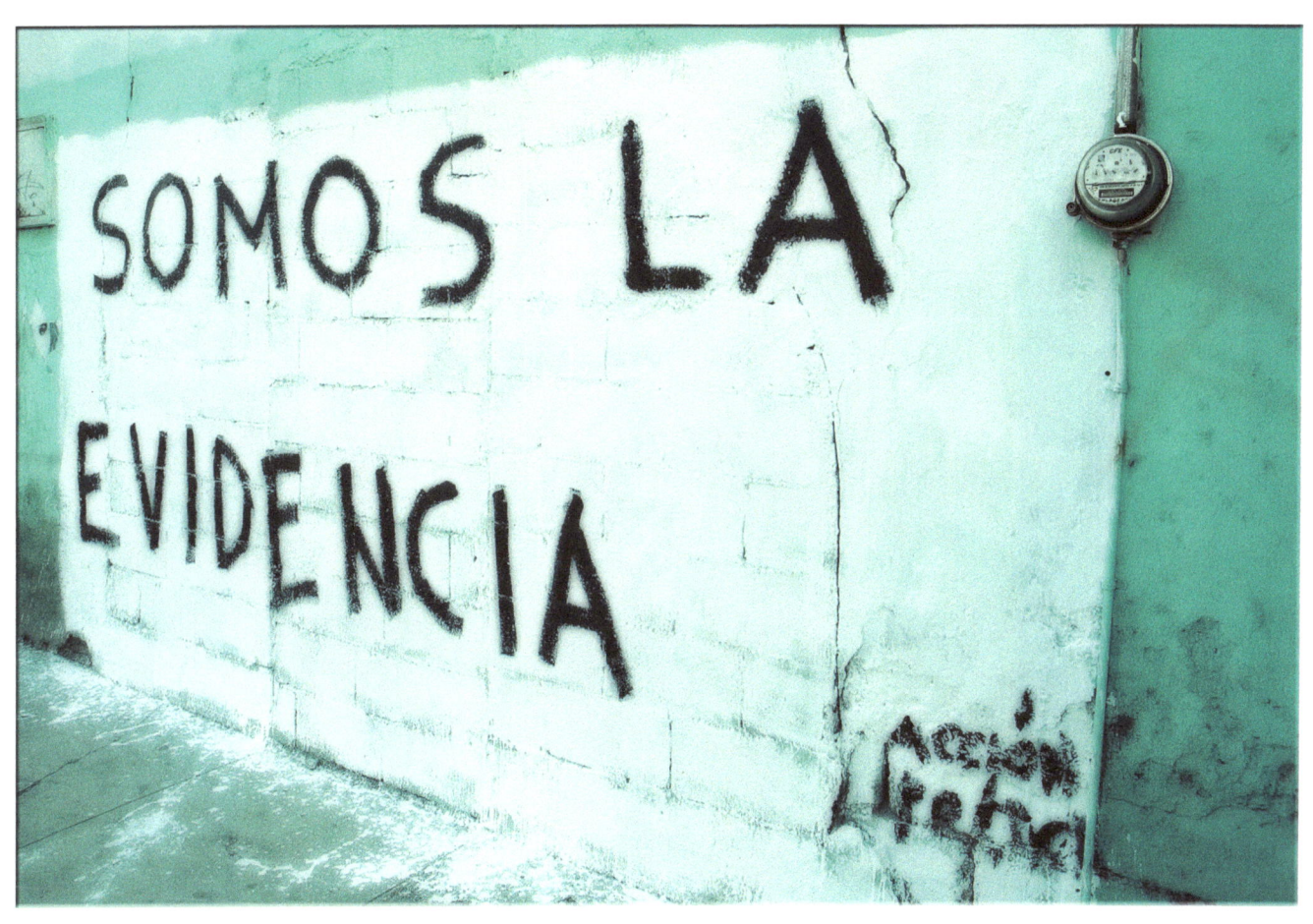

We are the evidence

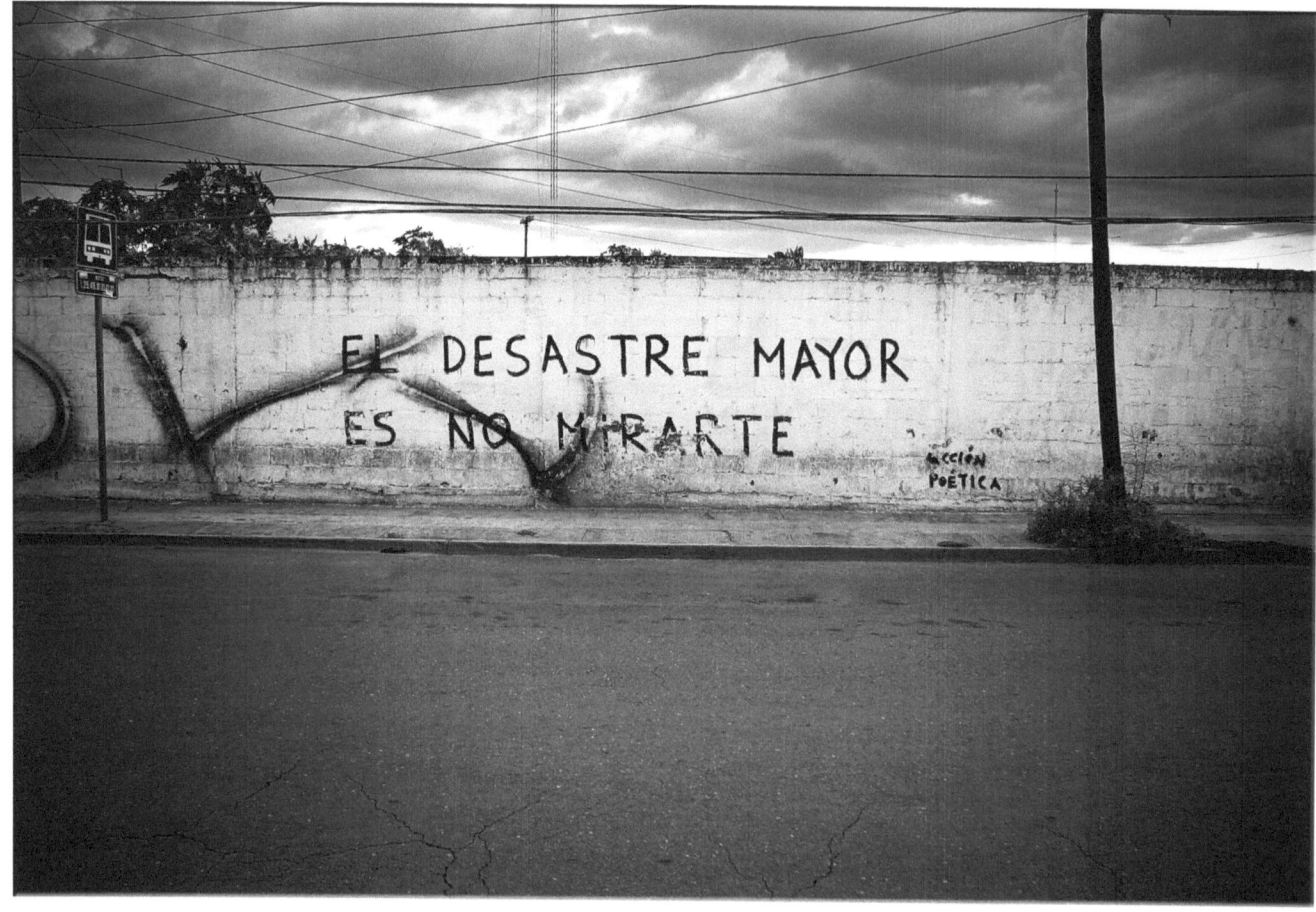

Not looking at you is the greatest disaster

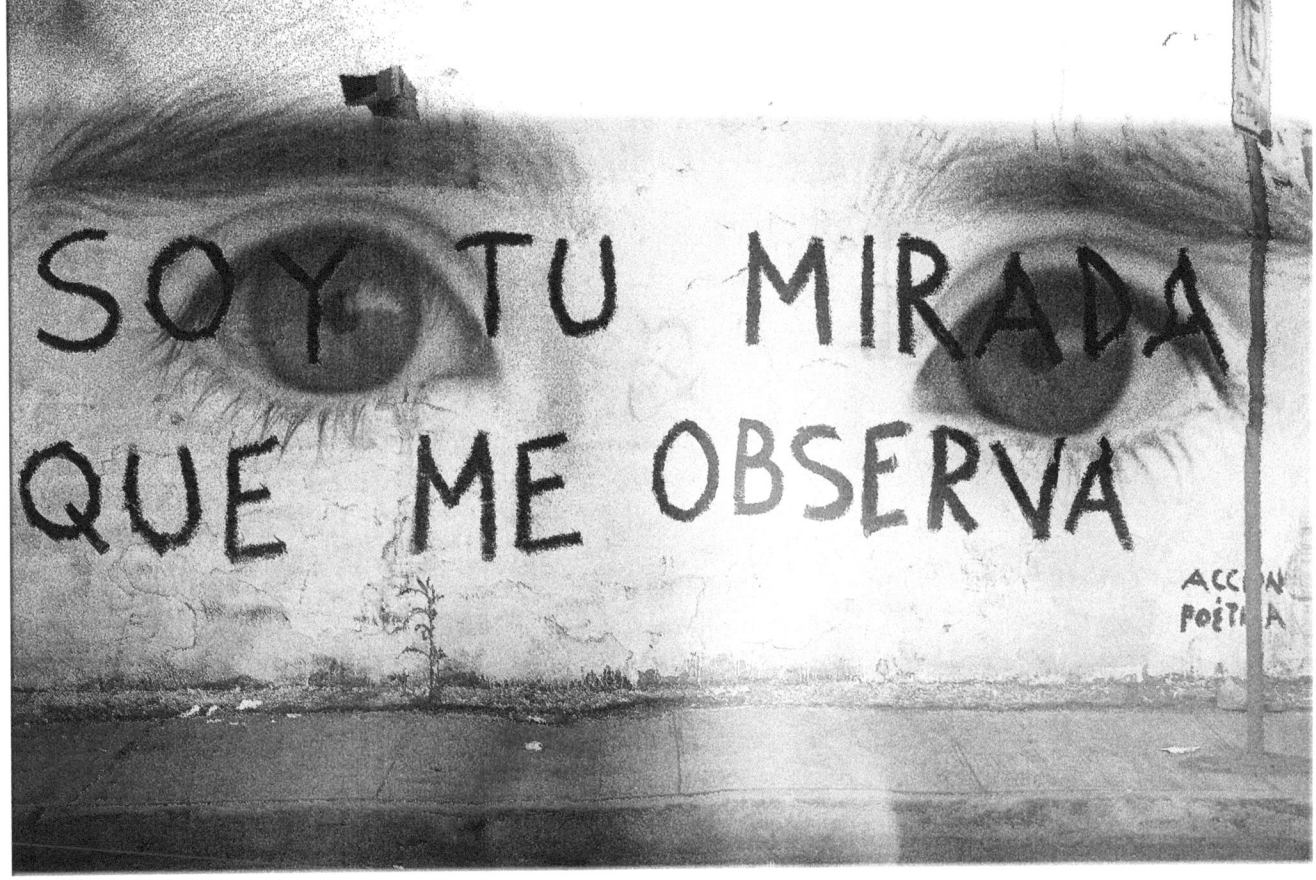

I am your gaze that observes me

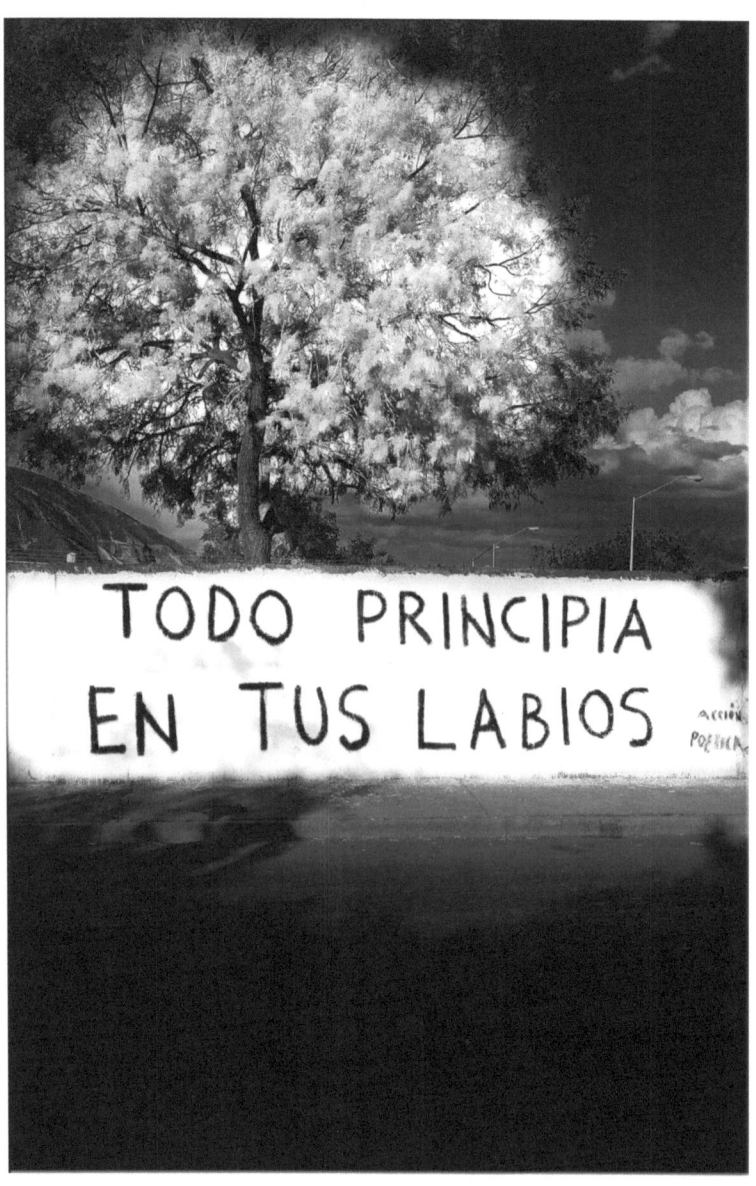

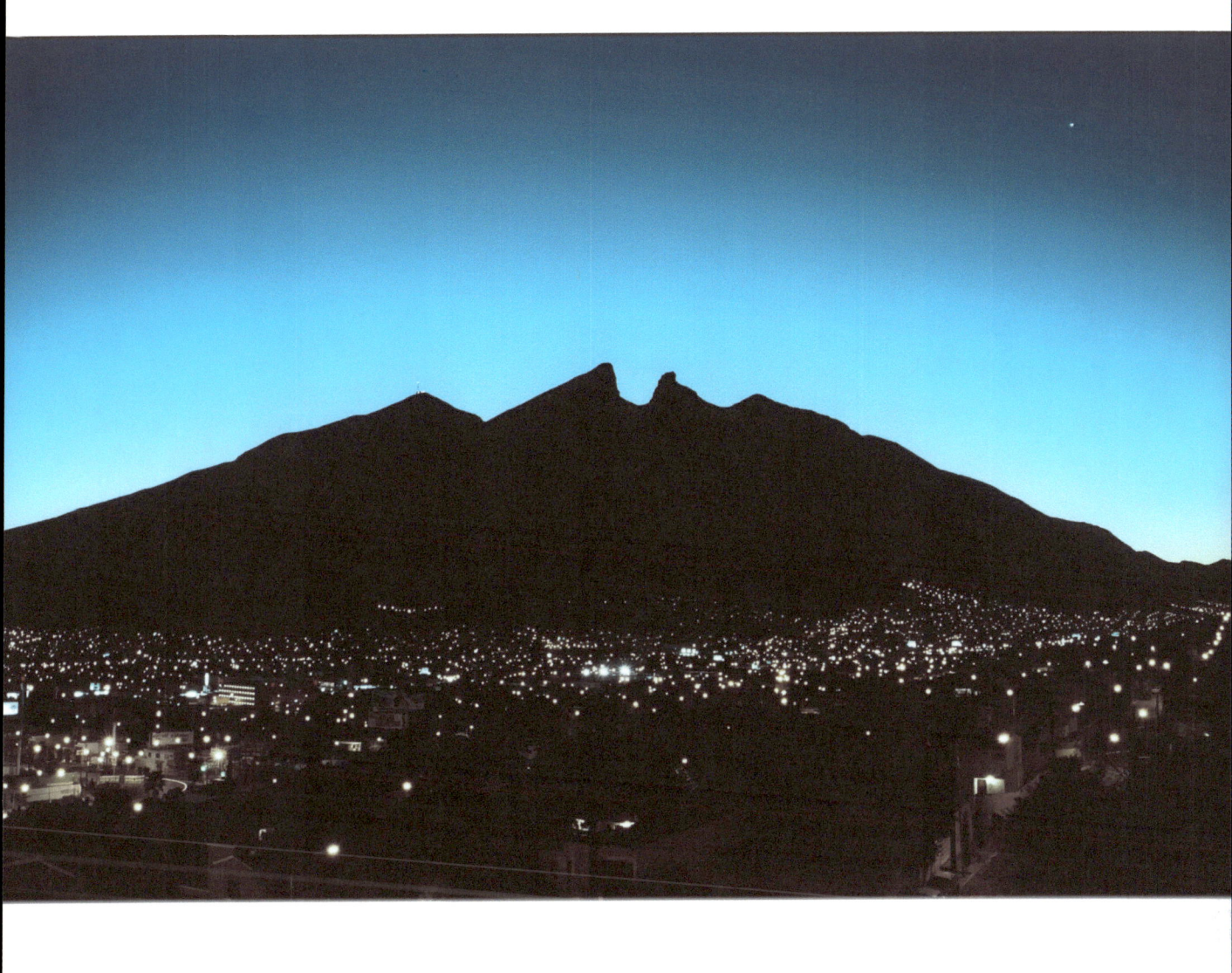

Sunrise, La Silla hill. Monterrey, Mexico.